EASY

Gourmet

impress for less

MURDOCH BOOKS

Having friends and family over for a meal is all about enjoying the moment: the company around you, the flavours on your plate and the pleasure of sharing your home and your table. These simple, budget-friendly recipes are tailor-made for entertaining. Thanks to clever combinations of ingredients, a few ingenious short cuts and some imaginative tips for presentation, these recipes turn everyday foods into elegant and enticing dishes, such as a classic potato and leek soup served just warm in teacups, or a delicate rice and rhubarb pudding served in old-fashioned glasses… delve into these pages and be inspired to share your table with our gorgeously simple feasts.

Contents

Starters

Hot vichyssoise with lemon cream and prawns • Buckwheat blinis with mushrooms • Baked ricotta with pancetta, tomato and olive salad • Asparagus, bean and egg salad with Thai coconut dressing • Roast fennel and feta rolls • Japanese clear noodle soup with clams and watercress • Baked parmesan custard with roast cauliflower and bacon salad • Fish, watercress and capsicum salad with paprika-walnut dressing • Chilled cucumber soup with curry oil • Linguine salad with radicchio, olives and basil • Pork rillettes with beetroot and cornichons • Lentil tapénade and roast capsicum toasts • Mushrooms baked with Taleggio, herbs and garlic crumbs • Rösti with smoked salmon and honey-mustard cream • Chicken liver pâté with port jelly and drunken figs • French onion soup with blue cheese toasts • Baked sardines with smoked paprika and thyme • Turkish toast with carrot-cumin purée and chickpea salad • Stuffed eggplant rolls with salsa verde • Green gazpacho with roast almonds • Dill puffs with mayonnaise and smoked trout • Braised spring vegetables with saffron aïoli • Crab cakes with ginger and sesame leaf salad • Rice, spinach and orange-stuffed calamari • Five-spice chicken wontons with ginger butter sauce • Prawn and avocado cocktail with chilli dressing • Tomato-feta tarts with lemon and oregano

✳ Preparation time: 10 minutes   **✳ Cooking time:** 55 minutes   **✳ Serves:** 4

Hot vichyssoise with lemon cream and prawns

60 g (2¼ oz/¼ cup) sour cream
½ teaspoon finely grated lemon rind
½ teaspoon lemon juice, or to taste
55 g (2 oz/¼ cup) butter
2 leeks, white part only, washed and
thinly sliced
2 tablespoons white wine
500 g (1 lb 2 oz/about 4) boiling potatoes,
peeled and chopped
450 ml (16 fl oz) vegetable or
chicken stock
250 ml (9 fl oz/1 cup) milk
2 tablespoons cream
8 large cooked king prawns (shrimp),
peeled, cleaned and chopped
1 tablespoon finely chopped chives

Combine the sour cream, lemon rind and juice in a small bowl, season to taste with sea salt and ground white pepper and set aside.

Melt the butter in a saucepan over low heat. Add the leek and cook, stirring often, for 10 minutes or until softened. Add the wine, potato and stock and bring to a simmer. Cook for 40 minutes or until the potato is very tender. Transfer the mixture to a food processor and process until smooth. Pass the soup through a fine strainer and return to a clean saucepan, warm the soup through over medium heat, then stir in the milk and cream. Season to taste. Heat for 1–2 minutes more, without allowing the soup to boil.

Divide the soup among 4 bowls or teacups and top each bowl with a few prawn pieces and a dollop of lemon cream mixture. Scatter over the chives and serve immediately.

Vichyssoise is a classic French soup, usually served cold. Serve our warmed up version in teacups and place any left-over soup in a pitcher on the table for top-ups.

Buckwheat blinis with mushrooms

Before you start cooking, thinly slice the spring onions and place them in a bowl of iced water until they curl. Drain well before using them as garnish.

35 g (1¼ oz/¼ cup) plain
   (all-purpose) flour
35 g (1¼ oz/¼ cup) buckwheat flour
3 teaspoons caster (superfine) sugar
½ teaspoon active dry yeast
125 ml (4 fl oz/½ cup) milk
25 g (1 oz) butter, chopped, plus extra
   melted butter, for cooking
1 large egg, lightly beaten
2 spring onions (scallions), thinly sliced,
   to garnish (*see tip*)

Mushroom topping
20 g (¾ oz) butter
750 g (1 lb 10 oz) Swiss brown
   mushrooms, thinly sliced
2 garlic cloves, crushed
1½ tablespoons lemon juice
125 g (4½ oz/½ cup) crème fraîche
   or sour cream
1 tablespoon thyme leaves,
   finely chopped

In a large bowl, combine the flours, sugar, yeast and ¼ teaspoon salt. Heat the milk and 25 g (1 oz) butter in a saucepan over low heat, stirring until the butter melts and the mixture is lukewarm. Add the milk mixture to the dry ingredients, whisking until smooth. Cover the batter with plastic wrap or a tea (dish) towel, leave in a draught-free, warm spot and allow to rise for 1–1½ hours or until doubled in size. Preheat the oven to 120°C (235°F/Gas ½).

Meanwhile, for the mushroom topping, melt the butter in a large frying pan over medium heat. Add the mushroom to the pan and cook, stirring often, for 10 minutes or until the mushrooms are starting to brown and all the liquid has evaporated. Add the garlic and lemon juice and cook for 1 minute. Remove the pan from the heat and stir in the crème fraîche and thyme. Set aside while the blinis cook.

Deflate the blini batter with a whisk and whisk in the egg.

Heat a large frying pan over medium heat and brush lightly with melted butter. Working in batches, add 60 ml (2 fl oz/¼ cup) cupfuls of batter to the pan and cook for 2–3 minutes or until bubbles appear on the surface. Turn the blinis and cook for 1 minute or until golden brown and cooked through. Transfer blinis as they cook to a warmed plate, cover loosely with foil and keep warm in the oven.

To serve, divide blinis among plates, top each with some of the mushroom mixture and decorate with spring onion curls.

Preparation time: 20 minutes
plus 1 hour 30 minutes for proving

Cooking time: 25 minutes

Serves: 6

Preparation time: 15 minutes   **Cooking time:** 40 minutes   **Serves:** 6–8

Baked ricotta with pancetta, tomato and olive salad

2 tablespoons olive oil, plus extra
  for greasing
2 tablespoons dried breadcrumbs
1 kg (2 lb 4 oz/4 cups) fresh, firm
  ricotta cheese
100 g (3½ oz/1 cup) parmesan
  cheese, grated
1 teaspoon grated lemon rind
½ teaspoon chilli flakes
1 egg yolk, lightly beaten
175 g (6 oz) thinly sliced pancetta
  (about 16 slices)
200 g (7 oz) mini roma (plum) tomatoes,
  halved lengthways
150 g (5½ oz/1 cup) pitted mixed olives
1 large handful wild rocket (arugula)
1 tablespoon balsamic vinegar (optional)

Preheat the oven to 180°C (350°F/Gas 4).

Lightly grease a 1 litre (35 fl oz/4 cup) capacity round ceramic dish with olive oil and dust with breadcrumbs, shaking out any excess. Combine the ricotta, parmesan, lemon rind, chilli and egg yolk in a large bowl. Season to taste with sea salt and freshly ground black pepper and stir to mix well. Spoon into the prepared dish and bake for 35–40 minutes or until golden and puffed. Cool slightly.

Meanwhile, place the pancetta on a baking tray and cook in the oven for 20 minutes or until crisp.

Put the tomatoes, olives, rocket, olive oil and balsamic vinegar, if using, in a bowl and toss to combine.

When the baked ricotta has cooled slightly, invert the dish onto a platter and cut into 6 or 8 wedges. Serve with the tomato and olive salad and crisp pancetta.

The ricotta can also be baked in individual serves. Simply grease six 175 ml (5½ fl oz/⅔ cup) capacity holes of a muffin tin and bake for 30 minutes in a 180°C (350°F/ Gas 4) oven.

Asparagus, bean and egg salad with Thai coconut dressing

2 handfuls coriander (cilantro) leaves,
  including roots
1½ teaspoons finely grated ginger
2 tablespoons sweet chilli sauce
2 teaspoons fish sauce
finely grated rind and juice of 1 lime
185 ml (6 fl oz/¾ cup) light coconut milk
1 teaspoon chilli flakes, or to taste
8 asparagus spears (about
  1 bunch), trimmed
200 g (7 oz/1⅔ cups) green beans
  or sugar snap peas, trimmed
225 g (8 oz/2½ cups) bean sprouts
1 small red onion, very thinly sliced
2 hard-boiled eggs, peeled and cut
  into wedges
50 g (1¾ oz/⅓ cup) coarsely chopped
  roasted peanuts (optional)

Remove the roots from the coriander and wash well, reserving the remaining coriander. Chop the roots finely, then combine in a food processor with the ginger, sweet chilli sauce, fish sauce, lime rind and juice, coconut milk and chilli flakes. Process until a smooth dressing forms, then season to taste with sea salt and freshly ground black pepper. Set aside.

Bring a saucepan of salted water to the boil. Cut the asparagus in half lengthways, then add to the boiling water with the beans, cover and cook for 2–3 minutes or until tender. Drain well, then rinse the vegetables under cold running water until cool. Drain well and pat dry using paper towels.

Trim the long stems from the coriander, then combine the coriander sprigs with the cooked vegetables, bean sprouts and onion in a large bowl. Add the dressing and toss gently to combine. Divide the salad among plates or bowls, scatter over the egg wedges and peanuts, if using, and serve immediately.

☀ Preparation time: 30 minutes　　**☀ Cooking time:** 10 minutes　　**☀ Serves:** 4

Preparation time: 30 minutes   Cooking time: 40 minutes   Serves: 4

Roast fennel and feta rolls

1 tablespoon extra virgin olive oil
1 rosemary sprig
1 fennel bulb (about 350 g/12 oz),
  trimmed and cut into 1 cm
  (½ inch) pieces
1 large red onion, cut into 1 cm
  (½ inch) pieces
185 ml (6 fl oz/¾ cup) chicken stock
75 g (2¾ oz/½ cup) crumbled feta cheese
1½ tablespoons chopped parsley
4 sheets filo pastry
50 g (1¾ oz) butter, melted
taramasalata, to serve (available from
  supermarkets and delis)

Heat the oil in a saucepan over medium heat, then add the rosemary, fennel and onion and stir to coat in the oil. Reduce the heat to low, cover and cook, stirring occasionally, for 10 minutes or until the vegetables begin to soften. Add the stock, bring to the boil over medium heat, cover, reduce the heat to low and cook for 10–15 minutes or until the vegetables are very soft and the liquid is absorbed. Cook, uncovered, to evaporate any excess liquid if necessary. Season to taste with sea salt and freshly ground black pepper, then cool. Remove the rosemary, then stir in the feta and parsley.

Preheat the oven to 190°C (375°F/Gas 5). Lay one sheet of filo on a clean work surface, keeping the remaining sheets covered with a damp cloth to prevent them drying out. Brush with some of the melted butter, then lay another sheet of filo on top. Cut the pastry in half lengthways, then in half widthways to give four even pieces. Brush each piece lightly with butter. Divide the filling into eight even portions, then place one portion evenly along a short side of one of the pieces of filo, leaving space at each end for folding. Fold the sides of the pastry over each end of the filling, then roll the pastry up to form a log. Repeat with the remaining filo, butter and filling, then transfer the rolls to a baking tray. Bake for 12–15 minutes or until golden and crisp. Divide the rolls among plates and serve with a spoonful of taramasalata on the side.

Fennel discolours quickly when exposed to the air. To prevent this, slip it into a bowl of cold water with 2 tablespoons of lemon juice added to it. Drain it well just before cooking. Instead of taramasalata, you could serve these rolls with baba ghanoush, if you prefer.

Japanese clear noodle soup with clams and watercress

You could use small, black mussels instead of clams or pipis; they will take about the same time to steam open.

6 dried shiitake mushrooms
1½ tablespoons ginger, washed and cut
  into thin matchsticks
2 teaspoons mirin
1–2 tablespoons light soy sauce, to taste
12 baby clams, or pipis, cleaned
135 g (4¾ oz) dried somen noodles
1 teaspoon sesame oil
1 spring onion (scallion), sliced diagonally
1 large handful watercress sprigs

Combine 1.5 litres (52 fl oz/6 cups) water and the shiitake mushrooms in a saucepan. Bring to the boil, cover, then reduce the heat and cook for 20 minutes or until the mushrooms are tender. Add the ginger, mirin and soy. Add the clams and cook for 2–3 minutes or just until they open. Remove the mushrooms and clams from the stock. When the mushrooms are cool enough to handle, trim the tough stems and slice the caps thinly. Return the mushroom slices to the liquid.

Cook the somen noodles in boiling water according to the packet instructions, then drain well.

Add the sesame oil to the broth. Divide the clams and noodles among shallow bowls, twisting the noodles into neat bundles, then gently ladle over the hot broth mixture. Garnish with the sliced spring onion and watercress sprigs.

Preparation time: 25 minutes   Cooking time: 30 minutes   Serves: 4

Preparation time: 20 minutes   **Cooking time:** 1 hour   **Serves:** 4

Baked parmesan custard with roast cauliflower and bacon salad

butter, for greasing
300 ml (10½ fl oz) cream
150 ml (5 fl oz) milk
2 dried bay leaves
75 g (2¾ oz/¾ cup) parmesan
  cheese, finely grated
2 eggs, plus 2 egg yolks

Roast cauliflower and bacon salad
½ a head (450 g/1 lb) cauliflower, cut
  into bite-sized florets (about 3½ cups)
2 tablespoons olive oil
115 g (4 oz) rashers rindless bacon
  (about 2), cut into 1 cm (½ inch) pieces
60 g (2¼ oz/½ cup) chopped walnuts
1 large handful flat-leaf (Italian) parsley
60 ml (2 fl oz/¼ cup) extra virgin olive oil
1 tablespoon sherry or red wine vinegar

Preheat the oven to 160°C (315°F/Gas 2–3). Grease four 170 ml (5½ fl oz/⅔ cup) ceramic moulds with butter and transfer to a baking dish.

Combine the cream, milk and bay leaves in a small saucepan and bring just to the boil. Remove from the heat, stir in the parmesan, then cool to room temperature. Whisk the whole eggs and yolks together in a bowl, then stir into the cream mixture to combine well. Season with salt to taste, then pour into the prepared moulds. Pour boiling water into the baking dish to come two-thirds up the sides of the moulds, then cover the moulds with foil. Bake for 30–35 minutes or until just firm to the touch. Remove the moulds from the water bath and set aside to cool to room temperature.

To make the roast cauliflower and bacon salad, increase oven temperature to 200°C (400°F/Gas 6). Toss the cauliflower in the oil and spread in a single layer in a roasting pan. Roast for 20–25 minutes or until tender and golden. Transfer to a bowl. Meanwhile, heat a non-stick frying pan over medium heat, add the bacon and cook, stirring, for 5–6 minutes or until crisp. Remove from the pan and drain on paper towel. Add the walnuts to the pan and cook for 2–3 minutes, tossing often, or until lightly toasted. Add the bacon, walnuts and parsley to the cauliflower. Combine the olive oil and vinegar in a jar and season to taste. Secure with the lid and shake well. Pour over the cauliflower and bacon salad and toss to coat well.

Run a knife around the edges of the custard moulds and invert onto serving plates, sprinkle with freshly ground black pepper and serve with cauliflower and bacon salad on the side.

The custards can be prepared in advance, covered and refrigerated for up to 12 hours. Bring to room temperature before serving.

Fish, watercress and capsicum salad with paprika-walnut dressing

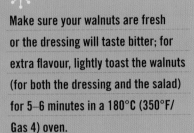

Make sure your walnuts are fresh or the dressing will taste bitter; for extra flavour, lightly toast the walnuts (for both the dressing and the salad) for 5–6 minutes in a 180°C (350°F/ Gas 4) oven.

500 g (1 lb 2 oz) new potatoes

80 ml (2½ fl oz/⅓ cup) olive oil, plus extra for cooking fish

2 red onions (about 300 g/10½ oz), peeled and cut into 1.5 cm (⅝ inch) thick wedges

2 red capsicums (peppers), trimmed, seeded and cut into 2 cm (¾ inch) wide strips

800 g (1 lb 12 oz) salmon fillets, or other oily fish fillets

2 handfuls watercress sprigs

40 g (1½ oz/⅓ cup) walnuts, coarsely chopped

Paprika-walnut dressing

2 garlic cloves, chopped

40 g (1½ oz/⅓ cup) walnuts, chopped (*see tip*)

2 teaspoons tomato paste (concentrated purée)

2 teaspoons honey

1 teaspoon smoked paprika

1 teaspoon dried oregano

50 ml (1¾ fl oz) red wine vinegar

160 ml (5¼ fl oz) extra virgin olive oil

To make the paprika-walnut dressing, combine all the ingredients except the olive oil in a food processor and process until a smooth paste forms. With the motor running, add the olive oil in a thin, steady stream and process until a smooth, thick dressing forms. Season to taste with sea salt and freshly ground black pepper and set aside.

Cook the potatoes in boiling, salted water for 15–20 minutes or until tender, then drain well. Cool to room temperature, then cut in half. Set aside.

Meanwhile, heat a chargrill pan over medium heat. Combine half the oil with the onion wedges in a bowl and toss to coat well. Chargrill the onions, in batches if necessary, for 3 minutes on each side or until slightly charred and tender, then set aside. Combine the capsicums and the remaining oil in a bowl and toss to coat well. Chargrill the capsicums, in batches if necessary, for 5–6 minutes, turning often, or until soft and charred around the edges, then set aside. Brush the fish all over with olive oil, then cook over medium–high heat for 2 minutes on each side, or until cooked but still a little pink in the middle. Cool, discard the skin, then flake the flesh coarsely, removing any bones.

To serve, place the capsicum, onion, potato, fish and watercress in a large bowl and toss gently until well combined. Divide among serving plates and scatter with the walnuts. Drizzle each with some of the dressing and serve any remaining dressing separately.

Preparation time: 30 minutes   Cooking time: 35 minutes   Serves: 6

Preparation time: 20 minutes
plus 2 hours chilling

Cooking time: 2 minutes

Serves: 4–6

Chilled cucumber soup with curry oil

3 telegraph (long) cucumbers, peeled,
seeded and coarsely chopped
3 spring onions (scallions), trimmed
and thinly sliced
1 garlic clove
125 g (4½ oz/½ cup) plain
Greek-style yoghurt
2 tablespoons lime juice
2 tablespoons sour cream
Tabasco sauce, to taste (optional)
185 ml (6 fl oz/¾ cup) chicken or
vegetable stock
1 small handful mint, chopped
290 ml (10 fl oz) vegetable oil
½ teaspoon curry powder
4 x 15 cm (6 inch) poppadoms

Combine the cucumber, onion, garlic, yoghurt, lime juice, sour cream, Tabasco, if using, stock and mint in a food processor and process until a smooth purée forms. Season to taste with sea salt and freshly ground black pepper, then transfer to a bowl, cover and refrigerate for 2 hours or until well chilled.

Heat 2 tablespoons of the vegetable oil in a small saucepan, add the curry powder and cook over medium heat for 30 seconds, or until fragrant, then cool.

Heat the remaining oil in a small frying pan until almost smoking. Add the poppadoms, in batches, and cook for 4–5 seconds or until puffed and golden. Remove with a slotted spoon and drain on paper towels. When cool enough to handle, roughly break into small pieces.

Serve the soup in bowls, drizzled with the curry oil and topped with poppadom pieces.

Linguine salad with radicchio, olives and basil

400 g (14 oz) linguine pasta
60 ml (2 fl oz/¼ cup) extra virgin olive oil,
  plus extra, to serve
2 small red onions, peeled and thinly
  sliced
95 g (3¼ oz/½ cup) chopped pitted
  kalamata olives
2 teaspoons finely grated lemon rind
60 ml (2 fl oz/¼ cup) lemon juice
2 garlic cloves, crushed
80 g (2¾ oz/1 cup) coarse breadcrumbs,
  made from day-old bread
2 tablespoons flat-leaf (Italian) parsley,
  coarsely chopped
1 large handful basil, thinly sliced,
  reserving 12 leaves to garnish
2 small or ½ large head of radicchio,
  leaves trimmed and thinly sliced
purchased tapénade, to serve (optional)

Cook the linguine in a large saucepan of salted, boiling water according to packet instructions or until al dente. Drain well in a colander, then combine in a large bowl with 1 tablespoon of the olive oil. Set aside.

Heat 1 tablespoon of the olive oil in a large frying pan over medium heat. Add the onion and cook, stirring, for 2–3 minutes or until starting to soften, then add the olives, lemon rind and juice and stir until well combined. Add to the pasta in the bowl.

Wipe the frying pan clean and heat the remaining olive oil over medium–high heat. Add the garlic and cook for 30 seconds or until golden. Add the breadcrumbs and cook, stirring often, for 3 minutes or until crumbs are golden. Remove from the heat and stir in the chopped parsley.

Add the basil and radicchio to the pasta mixture in the bowl, then season well with sea salt and freshly ground black pepper. Toss to combine well. Divide the salad among bowls. Drizzle with the extra virgin olive oil, sprinkle with garlic crumbs and garnish with basil leaves. Serve immediately with a little tapénade spooned over, if using.

Preparation time: 20 minutes   **Cooking time:** 15 minutes   **Serves:** 4–6

Preparation time: 30 minutes **Cooking time:** 5 hours **Serves:** 6

Pork rillettes with pickled beetroot and cornichons

1 kg (2 lb 4 oz) pork belly, rind and
  bones removed
100 g (3½ oz) pork back fat
1½ teaspoons salt
2 garlic cloves, crushed
125 ml (4 fl oz/½ cup) dry white wine
½ teaspoon feshly grated nutmeg
3 juniper berries, chopped
1 bay leaf
1 thyme sprig
baguette and cornichons, to serve

Pickled beetroot

375 g (13 oz) small beetroot (beets)
  (about 5), scrubbed and stems trimmed
60 ml (2 fl oz/¼ cup) balsamic vinegar
2 teaspoons caster (superfine) sugar
2 thyme sprigs
2 tablespoons extra virgin olive oil

Preheat the oven to 140°C (275°F/Gas 1). Cut pork belly and pork fat into 2 cm (¾ inch) strips. Combine in a casserole dish with the salt, garlic, wine, nutmeg, juniper berries, bay leaf and thyme. Cover tightly and bake for 4 hours or until the meat is very tender and has given up its fat. Remove the bay leaf and thyme, then pour the mixture into a strainer placed over a bowl. Drain the meat well, reserving the fat.

Transfer the warm pork to a large plate or clean board and using two forks, shred the pork. Place in a deep 1 litre (35 fl oz/4 cup) capacity terrine dish and smooth the surface. Melt the reserved pork fat and pour over the pork, then refrigerate until the fat is firm. Cover and store in the refrigerator for up to 1 week.

Meanwhile, to make the pickled beetroot, place the beetroot in a small saucepan over medium heat. Add 2 tablespoons of the vinegar, sugar, thyme and enough cold water to just cover. Bring to the boil, then reduce heat to low and cook for about 40 minutes or until tender. Drain the beetroot well, then cool slightly. When cool enough to handle, pull skins off the beetroot (you may wish to wear gloves to do this), then cool completely. Thinly slice the beetroot and combine in a bowl with the remaining vinegar and olive oil. Season to taste and toss to coat well.

Serve the rillettes at room temperature spread on the baguette, accompanied by the pickled beetroot and cornichons.

Rillettes is a French meat-based spread, traditionally made with pork or goose meat.

Lentil tapénade and roast capsicum toasts

1 large red capsicum (pepper), trimmed, seeded and cut into quarters

80 ml (2½ fl oz/⅓ cup) extra virgin olive oil, plus extra for brushing

12 x 7 mm (⅜ inch) thick slices of day-old baguette, cut on the diagonal

1 x 400 g (14 oz/2 cups) tin brown lentils, rinsed and drained well

2 garlic cloves, chopped

2 tablespoons capers, drained well

1 tablespoon chopped anchovy fillets

100 g (3½ oz/¾ cup) pitted black olives, chopped

2 teaspoons chopped oregano leaves

1 tablespoon lemon juice

150 g (5½ oz/about 3) bocconcini (fresh baby mozzarella cheese), thinly sliced (optional)

1 large handful baby rocket (arugula)

1 small handful mint leaves

Preheat the oven to 200°C (400°F/Gas 6). Place the capsicum in a roasting pan and drizzle with 1½ tablespoons of the olive oil. Roast for 25–30 minutes or until very soft and slightly charred around the edges. Remove from the dish, reserving any juices, place in a plastic bag and seal. When cool enough to handle, remove the skins and seeds. Cut into 2 cm (¾ inch) wide strips, combine in a bowl with reserved juices and set aside.

Place the slices of baguette on a baking tray in a single layer and brush lightly with olive oil. Bake for 10–12 minutes or until crisp and light golden, then transfer to a wire rack and cool.

Combine the remaining olive oil, lentils, garlic, capers, anchovies, olives, oregano and lemon juice in a food processor and process until a coarse purée forms. Season to taste with sea salt and freshly ground black pepper.

Add the bocconcini, if using, to the capsicum in the bowl and toss to combine well. Place 2 slices of baguette, overlapping, on a plate and top with a quarter of the capsicum mixture. Repeat with the remaining baguette slices and capsicum, then divide the lentil tapénade among plates, spooning it on top of the capsicum. Top with the rocket and mint leaves and serve immediately.

Preparation time: 25 minutes   **Cooking time:** 40 minutes   **Serves:** 6

Preparation time: 15 minutes   **Cooking time:** 30 minutes   **Serves:** 4

Mushrooms baked with Taleggio, herbs and garlic crumbs

1 tablespoon olive oil

8 (about 850 g/1 lb 14 oz) medium-large flat mushrooms, peeled

60 g (2¼ oz) butter, melted

½ leek, white part only, washed and thinly sliced

2 garlic cloves, finely chopped

2 tablespoons white wine

100 g (3½ oz/1¼ cups) fresh breadcrumbs

1 teaspoon thyme leaves

1 tablespoon flat-leaf (Italian) parsley, finely chopped, plus whole leaves, to serve

200 g (7 oz) Taleggio cheese, cut into 8 even slices

Preheat the oven to 180°C (350°F/Gas 4). Brush a baking tray with the oil. Remove the stems from the mushrooms. Finely chop the stems and set the caps aside.

Heat 40 g (1½ oz) of the butter in a small frying pan over low heat and add the leek, garlic and mushroom stems. Cook, stirring often, for 5 minutes or until softened, then add the wine and cook for 3 minutes. Remove from the heat and place in a bowl, add the breadcrumbs, herbs and remaining butter. Season to taste with sea salt and freshly ground black pepper and mix well.

Place the mushroom caps on the prepared baking tray in a single layer, cap side up. Fill each cap with a slice of Taleggio cheese, then divide the crumb mixture evenly among the mushrooms. Bake for 20 minutes, or until the mushrooms are tender and golden. Serve warm topped with parsley leaves.

For a slightly more sophisticated table setting, mix your everyday crockery with something a little more ornate by serving these mushrooms on a lovely vintage platter.

Rösti with smoked salmon and honey-mustard cream

800 g (1 lb 12 oz) desiree potatoes
  (about 4)
1 egg, lightly beaten
60 ml (2 fl oz/¼ cup) vegetable oil
200 g (7 oz) sliced smoked salmon
1 tablespoon chives, cut into 1 cm
  (½ inch) pieces

Honey-mustard cream
60 g (2¼ oz/¼ cup) sour cream
1 teaspoon wholegrain mustard
1 teaspoon lemon juice
½ teaspoon honey

To make the honey-mustard cream, combine all the ingredients in a small bowl. Add about 2 teaspoons of water to make a drizzling consistency, then cover and refrigerate until ready to serve.

Preheat the oven to 120°C (235°F/Gas ½). Peel the potatoes and coarsely grate. Place the grated potato in a clean tea (dish) towel and gently squeeze out any excess moisture. Place into a bowl and combine with the egg. Season to taste with sea salt and freshly ground black pepper.

Heat the oil in a large frying pan over medium heat. Cook the potato mixture in batches, using 60 ml (2 fl oz/¼ cup) of the mixture for each rösti, flattening out to make rounds about 8 cm (3¼ inches) across. Cook for 5–6 minutes, turning once, or until golden and cooked through. Transfer to a plate, cover loosely with foil and keep warm in the oven while the remaining mixture cooks.

To serve, top the rösti with salmon slices, drizzle with the honey-mustard cream and sprinkle with chives.

Preparation time: 15 minutes   **Cooking time:** 15 minutes   **Serves:** 4

✳ **Preparation time:** 60 minutes
plus chilling

✳ **Cooking time:** 45 minutes

✳ **Serves:** 6

Chicken liver pâté with port jelly and drunken figs

350 g (12 oz) chicken livers, trimmed
100 g (3½ oz) butter
2 French shallots, finely chopped
1 garlic clove, crushed
¼ teaspoon ground allspice
2 tablespoons port
80 ml (2½ fl oz/⅓ cup) cream
1 egg white
1 baguette

Port jelly
60 ml (2 fl oz/¼ cup) port
1 teaspoon powdered gelatine

Drunken figs
180 g (6 oz) dried figs (about 12)
185 ml (6 fl oz/¾ cup) port
½ cinnamon stick

Pat the livers dry with a paper towel. Melt 30 g (1 oz) of the butter in a frying pan and add the shallots and garlic. Cook, stirring, over low heat for about 5 minutes or until soft. Increase heat to medium, add the livers and allspice, and cook, stirring, for 1 minute, then add the port and cook for 30 seconds; take care not to overcook the livers or the pâté will be grainy. Remove from the heat and cool slightly.

Combine the liver mixture and the remaining butter in a food processor and season well with sea salt and freshly ground black pepper. Process until smooth, then cool to room temperature. Whisk the cream in a small bowl until soft peaks form, then fold into the liver mixture. Using clean beaters, whisk the egg white in a small bowl until soft peaks form and fold into the liver mixture. Carefully spoon the mixture into six 250 ml (9 fl oz/1 cup) capacity ramekins, cover and refrigerate until firm.

To make the port jelly, combine the port and 60 ml (2 fl oz/¼ cup) water in a small, heatproof cup. Sprinkle the gelatine over the top and stand until the gelatine is softened. Stand cup in a saucepan of simmering water and stir until the gelatine has dissolved, then cool. Pour the port mixture over the liver mixture and allow to set.

To make the drunken figs, combine the figs, port, cinnamon stick and 60 ml (2 fl oz/¼ cup) water in a small saucepan. Bring to the boil, reduce the heat to low, then cook, uncovered, for 15 minutes or until the figs are soft and the liquid is reduced and syrupy. Cool.

Preheat the oven to 150°C (300°F/Gas 2). Thinly slice the baguette on the diagonal. Place in a single layer on baking trays and bake for 20 minutes or until crisp and dry; cool, then use immediately or store in an airtight container. Toasts can be made up to 2 days in advance. Serve the chicken liver pâté with the drunken figs and toasted baguette.

The pâté will keep refrigerated for 2-3 days. The drunken figs will keep refrigerated in an airtight container for up to 1 week.

French onion soup with blue cheese toasts

30 g (1 oz) butter
1 tablespoon olive oil
2 kg (4 lb 8 oz) onions, thinly sliced
500 ml (17 fl oz/2 cups) sweet sherry
1.25 litres (44 fl oz/5 cups) chicken stock
½ baguette
50 g (1¾ oz) mild blue cheese

Heat the butter and oil in a large saucepan over medium heat for 2–3 minutes or until the butter has melted. Add the onions and cook, stirring often, for 20–25 minutes or until the onions are very soft and starting to caramelise. Add the sherry, bring to the boil and cook for 1 minute, scraping the bottom of the pan with a wooden spoon to remove any cooked-on pieces of onion. Add the chicken stock and return the mixture to the boil for 3–4 minutes. Reduce heat to very low, cover the saucepan and cook for 1 hour.

Preheat the oven grill (broiler) to medium. Just before serving, slice baguette into eight 5 mm (¼ inch) thick slices; you may not need all the baguette. Place slices of bread on a baking tray and grill (broil) for 1–2 minutes or until lightly toasted. Remove toasts, turn over and spread with blue cheese. Grill the toasts for another 2–3 minutes or until the edges are golden and cheese is bubbling.

Divide the soup among serving bowls, top each with 2 cheese toasts and serve immediately.

Preparation time: 30 minutes   **Cooking time:** 1 hour 40 minutes   **Serves:** 4

Preparation time: 15 minutes   **Cooking time:** 10 minutes   **Serves:** 4

Baked sardines with smoked paprika and thyme

12 butterflied sardine fillets
olive oil, for greasing
lemon wedges, to serve

Stuffing
80 g (2¾ oz/1 cup) fresh breadcrumbs
2 tablespoons chopped flat-leaf
  (Italian) parsley
1 tablespoon chopped thyme leaves
2 garlic cloves, finely chopped
½ teaspoon smoked paprika
1½ tablespoons extra virgin olive oil,
  plus extra, to serve

Preheat the oven to 220°C (425°F/Gas 7).

For the stuffing, combine all the ingredients in a bowl.

Arrange the sardines, skin side down, on a baking tray lined with lightly oiled baking paper. Take half of the stuffing and divide between the sardines. Pat mixture over the surface of one side of each fillet and fold the other side over to cover the stuffing. Crumble remaining stuffing over the sardines and season with sea salt and freshly ground black pepper. Bake for 8 minutes or until crumbs are golden.

Drizzle with a little extra oil and serve immediately with lemon wedges on the side.

Turkish toast with carrot-cumin purée and chickpea salad

140 g (5 oz/⅔ cup) dried chickpeas
   (garbanzo beans)
600 g (1 lb 5 oz) carrots (about 4),
   peeled and coarsely chopped
1 teaspoon sweet paprika
1½ teaspoons ground cumin
1 large handful coriander (cilantro)
   leaves, chopped
80 ml (2½ fl oz/⅓ cup) lemon juice
large pinch cayenne pepper, or to taste
200 ml (7 fl oz) olive oil
1 medium eggplant (aubergine)
   (about 325 g/11½ oz), trimmed and
   cut into 2 cm (¾ inch) pieces
2 large tomatoes (about 360 g/12¾ oz)
   trimmed and cut into 2 cm
   (¾ inch) pieces
1 small handful parsley, chopped
1 loaf Turkish bread

Soak chickpeas overnight in enough cold water to cover, then drain well. Place chickpeas in a saucepan and cover with water. Bring to the boil and cook over medium–high heat for about 1½ hours or until tender, adding extra water to keep chickpeas covered as necessary. Drain well.

Meanwhile, place the carrots in a saucepan and cover with water. Bring to the boil and cook for about 30 minutes or until very soft, then drain well. Transfer to a food processor, add the paprika, 1 teaspoon of the cumin, half the coriander and lemon juice, cayenne pepper and 80 ml (2½ fl oz/⅓ cup) of the olive oil. Season to taste with sea salt and freshly ground black pepper, then cool to room temperature.

Heat 80 ml (2½ fl oz/⅓ cup) of the olive oil in a frying pan over medium heat. Carefully add the eggplant pieces and cook slowly, turning often for 15–20 minutes or until very soft and deep golden, adding a little more oil if necessary. Transfer mixture to a colander placed over a bowl to drain, reserving pan juices. Measure 30 ml (1 fl oz) of the reserved pan juices and return them to the frying pan. Heat over low heat, add remaining cumin and cook for 1 minute or until mixture foams. Add tomato, season to taste and cook over medium heat, stirring often, for 5 minutes or until softened. Add the eggplant, parsley and remaining coriander and lemon juice, then stir in the chickpeas.

Heat the oven to 200°C (400°F/Gas 6). Slice turkish bread on the diagonal into thin slices. Brush with remaining olive oil and place in a single layer on a baking tray. Bake until bread is golden.

Serve carrot purée with toasted Turkish bread and chickpea salad.

Preparation time: 25 minutes
plus 20 minutes standing time

Cooking time: 55 minutes

Serves: 4

Stuffed eggplant rolls with salsa verde

1 large eggplant (aubergine)
(about 675 g/1 lb 8 oz), trimmed
2 tablespoons sea salt
3 small (375 g/13 oz) washed potatoes,
peeled and chopped
185 ml (6 fl oz/¾ cup) olive oil
75 g (2¾ oz/¾ cup) grated
parmesan cheese
185 g (6½ oz/¾ cup) firm fresh
ricotta cheese
2 egg yolks
½ teaspoon freshly grated nutmeg

Salsa verde
2 large handfuls flat-leaf (Italian) parsley
1 small handful mint
1 tablespoon capers, rinsed and drained
3 anchovy fillets, drained
2 garlic cloves, chopped
1 tablespoon dijon mustard
2 tablespoons lemon juice
125 ml (4 fl oz/½ cup) good-quality
extra virgin olive oil

Tomato salad
1 vine-ripened tomato
40 g (1½ oz/⅓ cup) hazelnuts, roasted
and chopped
1 small handful basil leaves

Cut the eggplant lengthways into eight 5 mm (¼ inch) thick slices. Discard end slices. Layer slices in a colander, sprinkle each layer with salt and stand for 20 minutes. Rinse and pat dry with paper towels.

Place the potatoes in saucepan and cover with cold water. Bring to the boil and cook for 7–10 minutes or until tender. Drain thoroughly, then mash with half the oil and half the parmesan. Transfer to a bowl to cool, then add ricotta, egg yolks and nutmeg and season to taste with sea salt and freshly ground black pepper.

Heat a large heavy-based frying pan over medium heat. Brush the eggplant slices with the remaining oil and season with pepper. Fry eggplant in batches for 2–3 minutes on each side or until golden and tender. Transfer to a plate. Preheat oven to 180°C (350°F/Gas 4). Lay eggplant slices on a clean work surface and spoon 2 heaped tablespoons of the potato filling widthways across the centre of each slice. Roll to enclose filling and transfer to a lightly oiled baking dish, seam side down. Sprinkle rolls with remaining parmesan and bake for 25–35 minutes or until golden.

For the salsa verde, place all ingredients except for the oil in the bowl of a food processor. Process until combined. Gradually add the oil with the motor running, process until smooth and season to taste.

For the salad, bring a small saucepan of water to the boil. Cut a cross in the base of the tomato and boil for 2 minutes. Place in cold water. Peel away skin, cut into quarters, remove seeds and finely chop flesh. Combine with nuts and basil. Place 2 eggplant rolls on each serving plate, top with salsa verde and serve with salad.

The rolls can be made as early as the night before and refrigerated. Reheat, covered with foil, in a 160°C (315°F/Gas 2–3) oven or serve at room temperature.

Green gazpacho with roast almonds

The amount of garlic you use will vary according to the size of the cloves. If these are very large, use only two, but if they are small, use four.

2–4 garlic cloves, chopped (*see tip*)
3 spring onions (scallions), trimmed
  and chopped
2 Lebanese (short) cucumbers (about
  350 g/12 oz), peeled and chopped
1 green capsicum (pepper)
  (about 250 g/9 oz), seeded and chopped
80 g (2¾ oz) day-old bread, chopped
½ an iceberg lettuce, outer leaves
  discarded, chopped
2 large handfuls flat-leaf (Italian)
  parsley, chopped
1 large handful coriander
  (cilantro) leaves, chopped
310–375 ml (10¾–13 fl oz/1¼–1½ cups)
  chicken stock
250 ml (9 fl oz/1 cup) extra virgin olive oil
60 ml (2 fl oz/¼ cup) sherry vinegar,
  or to taste
80 g (2 ¾ oz/1½ cup) roasted almonds,
  coarsely chopped

Combine the garlic, spring onion, cucumber, capsicum, bread, lettuce and herbs in a large bowl. Working in batches, process the mixture in a food processor, adding a little of the chicken stock to each batch, until a purée forms. Transfer the purée to a large bowl, then stir in 185 ml (6 fl oz/¾ cup) of the olive oil and the sherry vinegar. Season to taste with sea salt and freshly ground black pepper. Cover the bowl tightly, then refrigerate for 2 hours or until well chilled. Divide soup among bowls and serve sprinkled with chopped almonds and drizzled with remaining olive oil.

Preparation time: 20 minutes
plus 2 hours chilling

cooking time: nil

Serves: 6

❋ **Preparation time:** 30 minutes   ❋ **Cooking time:** 30 minutes   ❋ **Serves:** 6
(makes 12 puffs)

Dill puffs with mayonnaise and smoked trout

Dill puffs

50 g (1¾ oz) unsalted butter, chopped

65 g (2½ oz) plain (all-purpose) flour, sifted

2 eggs

50 g (1¾ oz/½ cup) finely grated parmesan cheese

2 teaspoons chopped dill

1 egg yolk lightly beaten with 1 tablespoon milk, to glaze

1 hot-smoked river trout (about 250 g/9 oz), skin and bones removed, flaked

1 handful watercress sprigs

Mayonnaise

125 g (4½ oz/½ cup) whole-egg mayonnaise

2 hard-boiled eggs, peeled and chopped

1 teaspoon lemon juice

1 tablespoon finely chopped dill

2 teaspoons capers, drained, rinsed and chopped

To make the mayonnaise, combine all ingredients in a bowl. Season with sea salt and freshly ground black pepper, cover and chill.

Preheat oven to 200°C (400°F/Gas 6). Line 2 baking trays with baking paper. Draw 6 circles 5 cm (2 inches) in diameter on each tray.

To make the dill puffs, combine 125 ml (4 fl oz/½ cup) water, butter and a pinch of salt in a saucepan over medium–high heat and bring to the boil. Immediately when butter has melted, remove from heat and add flour. Working quickly, stir mixture vigorously with a wooden spoon until smooth. Return pan to medium heat and cook, stirring constantly, for 3 minutes or until mixture comes away from the sides of the pan and forms a ball. Remove from heat. Stir the eggs into the mixture, one at a time, ensuring each is incorporated and the mixture comes away from the sides of the pan before adding the next. Stir in parmesan, reserving 1 tablespoon, and dill.

Spoon or pipe dough using a medium-sized plain tube onto prepared trays, covering the circles with the mixture. Brush tops with egg glaze and sprinkle over reserved parmesan. Bake for 10 minutes or until puffed, then reduce heat to 180°C (350°F/Gas 4) and bake a further 15 minutes until golden brown; do not open oven door while puffs are baking. Transfer puffs to a wire rack. Working quickly, carefully pierce the base of each hot puff with a small, sharp knife to release steam. Using a serrated knife, halve each puff horizontally.

Lift the top off each puff, divide trout between puffs, then top trout with a heaped teaspoon of mayonnaise and a sprig of watercress. Replace top half of puff gently and serve immediately.

Puffs can be made ahead and stored in an airtight container for up to 2 days. Reheat in a 180°C (350°F/ Gas 4) oven for 5 minutes to crisp before serving.

Braised spring vegetables with saffron aïoli

1 tablespoon extra virgin olive oil

6 pickling onions, peeled and quartered

1 rasher bacon, rind removed, finely
  chopped (optional)

2 garlic cloves, finely chopped

4 small thyme sprigs, plus extra,
  to serve

125 ml (4 fl oz/½ cup) white wine

375 ml (13 fl oz/1½ cups) chicken stock

1 desiree potato (about 170 g/6 oz), cut
  into 1 cm (½ inch) pieces

350 g (12 oz) baby carrots (about
  1 bunch), peeled and trimmed

6 spears (about 1 bunch) asparagus,
  trimmed and halved lengthways

150 g (5½ oz/1 cup) frozen broad (fava)
  beans, thawed and peeled

80 g (2¾ oz/½ cup) frozen peas

Saffron aïoli

1 large pinch saffron threads

125 g (4½ fl oz/½ cup)
  whole-egg mayonnaise

1 garlic clove, finely chopped

For the saffron aïoli, sprinkle saffron over 2 tablespoons of hot water in a cup and stand for 1 hour or until liquid is deep yellow. Place saffron liquid, mayonnaise and garlic in a small bowl and stir to combine well. Cover and set aside.

Heat olive oil in a large heavy-based saucepan over medium–low heat. Add the onions and cook, stirring often, for 4–6 minutes. Increase the heat to medium and add the bacon, if using, garlic and thyme. Cook for another 3–4 minutes, then add white wine and stock. Add the potato and carrots. Bring to the boil and reduce heat to low. Simmer, covered for 10–12 minutes or until vegetables are just tender. Remove the lid, add the asparagus and cook for 2 minutes. Add the broad beans and peas and cook for 1 minute or until beans and peas are tender. Remove thyme and season to taste. Ladle into bowls and serve topped with thyme sprigs and saffron aïoli on the side.

Preparation time: 25 minutes
plus 1 hour standing time

Cooking time: 25 minutes

Serves: 4–6

Preparation time: 25 minutes
plus 30 minutes chilling

Cooking time: 20 minutes

Serves: 6

Crab cakes with ginger and sesame leaf salad

1 tablespoon pickled ginger, thinly sliced
1 tablespoon light soy sauce
2 teaspoons finely grated ginger
60 ml (2 fl oz/¼ cup) sesame oil
30 ml (1 fl oz) rice wine vinegar
1 teaspoon caster (superfine) sugar
2 teaspoons sesame seeds, lightly toasted
300 g (10½ oz) waxy potatoes such as
  desiree, peeled and chopped
1 x 510 g (1 lb 2 oz) tin crabmeat, drained
3 spring onions (scallions), trimmed and
  thinly sliced
35 g (1¼ oz/¼ cup) plain
  (all-purpose) flour
3 eggs, lightly beaten
60 g (2¼ oz/1 cup) panko
  crumbs (Japanese breadcrumbs)
250 ml (9 fl oz/1 cup) vegetable oil
2 large handfuls mixed baby
  salad leaves, to serve

Combine the pickled ginger, soy, ginger, sesame oil, rice wine vinegar and sugar in a small bowl and whisk to combine. Stir in the sesame seeds, then set aside.

Place potatoes in a saucepan and cover with cold water. Bring to the boil and simmer for 7–10 minutes or until tender. Drain well, then mash until smooth. Add the crabmeat and spring onion, season to taste with sea salt and freshly ground black pepper and mix until well combined. Divide the mixture into six even portions, then shape each into a round, 8 cm (3¼ inch) cake. Cover and refrigerate for 15 minutes or until firm.

Place the flour, eggs and panko crumbs into 3 separate shallow bowls. Working with one at a time, place a crab cake into the flour, shaking off any excess, then into the egg, draining off excess and then into the crumbs, patting crumbs on firmly to coat. Place the crumbed cakes on a plate lined with baking paper and place in the refrigerator for 15 minutes or until firm.

Heat the oil in a large, deep frying pan over medium heat. Cook the crab cakes for 4 minutes on each side or until golden.

Place salad leaves in a bowl and toss gently with half the dressing. Divide salad evenly among serving plates, top with crab cakes, drizzle over remaining dressing and serve immediately.

Rice, spinach and orange-stuffed calamari

65 g (2½ oz/⅓ cup) long-grain rice
6 x 120 g (4¼ oz) fresh calamari
2 oranges
100 ml (3½ fl oz) extra virgin olive oil
1 red onion, finely chopped
2 garlic cloves, crushed
2½ tablespoons currants
1 large handful baby spinach
  leaves, chopped
1 small fennel bulb, with fronds, shaved

Cook rice in plenty of boiling, lightly salted water for 15–20 minutes or until tender. Drain well then cool.

Clean the calamari, leaving the hoods whole and reserving the tentacles. Remove skin, beak and wings from hoods, discarding skin. Wash the calamari, then drain well and pat dry with paper towels. Chop the tentacles and wings finely.

Finely grate the rind of 1 orange, avoiding any white pith. Juice the orange, then strain juice. Heat 2 tablespoons of the oil in a small saucepan over low heat. Add half the grated orange rind and stand over low heat for 2–3 minutes. Remove from the heat and stand for 10–15 minutes to infuse. Strain well, then set aside.

Heat 2 tablespoons of the remaining oil in a large frying pan over medium heat, then add onion, garlic, currants and chopped tentacles and wings. Cook, stirring, for 2–3 minutes or until onion and calamari have softened. Add the chopped spinach leaves, strained orange juice and remaining rind. Cook for another 2–3 minutes or until spinach is wilted. Stir in the rice and cook for 2–3 minutes or until the juice has been absorbed. Cool.

Stuff the calamari tubes firmly but not too tightly with the mixture and secure ends with a toothpick. Heat remaining oil in a clean frying pan over medium heat. Cook the calamari for 6 minutes, turning frequently, or until calamari is tender and stuffing is heated through.

Segment remaining orange and combine with shaved fennel and fronds. To serve, remove toothpicks from calamari and cut each tube in half widthways on a slight diagonal. Divide among plates. Gently reheat the orange-infused oil, then drizzle over the calamari and serve immediately with orange-fennel salad.

Preparation time: 30 minutes
plus 10–15 minutes standing time

Cooking time: 40 minutes

Serves: 4–6

Preparation time: 45 minutes
plus 20 minutes soaking

Cooking time: 15 minutes

Serves: 4

Five-spice chicken wontons with ginger butter sauce

3 dried shiitake mushrooms
250 g (9 oz) minced (ground) chicken
2 tablespoons tinned water chestnuts
  (about 2), drained and chopped
2 tablespoons tinned bamboo shoots,
  drained and chopped
¾ teaspoon Chinese five-spice powder
2 teaspoons soy sauce
½ teaspoon sesame oil
1 tablespoon cornflour (cornstarch)
270 g (9½ oz) packet Shanghai
  wonton wrappers

Ginger butter sauce
125 g (4½ oz) butter
1½ tablespoons ginger, cut into
  fine matchsticks
1 spring onion (scallion), trimmed
  and sliced on the diagonal
Chinese black vinegar, to serve
  (optional)

Place the dried mushrooms in a heatproof bowl, cover with boiling water and soak for 20 minutes, or until softened. Drain well, discard stems, then finely chop mushrooms and place in a bowl with the minced chicken, water chestnuts, bamboo shoots, five-spice powder, soy sauce, sesame oil and cornflour and mix well using your hands.

For the wontons, place about 1 tablespoon of the mixture onto the centre of 12 wonton wrappers, flattening slightly. Brush the edges with water to moisten and top with remaining wrappers. Press edges together firmly to seal well.

To cook the wontons, bring a large saucepan of water to the boil then cook, in batches if necessary, for 4–5 minutes, or until wontons rise to the top. Remove from the water using a slotted spoon and drain well.

While the wontons are cooking, make the butter sauce. Melt the butter in a small saucepan over medium–low heat, then simmer for 4–5 minutes or until golden and foamy. Add the ginger and spring onion and cook for 1 minute or until the mixture is fragrant.

To serve, divide the wontons among warmed plates, drizzle with the ginger butter sauce and Chinese black vinegar, if using, and serve immediately.

Wontons can be made 4–6 hours in advance. Place on a baking paper-lined baking tray, cover with plastic wrap and refrigerate until ready to cook.

Prawn and avocado cocktail with chilli dressing

The chilli dressing can be made ahead of time but do not add the tomato and prawns until just before serving. The cocktail does not keep well once assembled. The lettuce needs to be very crisp and fresh.

1 large firm, ripe avocado
   (about 300 g/10½ oz)
50 ml (1½ fl oz) lemon juice
550 g (1 lb 4 oz) cooked king prawns
   (shrimp), peeled and cleaned or 250 g
   (9 oz) cooked prawn (shrimp) meat,
   cut into 1 cm (½ inch) slices
1 small roma (plum) tomato (about
   100 g/3½ oz), finely chopped and
   seeds removed
4 large iceberg lettuce leaves, trimmed,
   washed and dried well

Chilli dressing

60 g (2¼ oz/¼ cup)
   whole-egg mayonnaise
1 tablespoon sour cream
2 teaspoons horseradish cream
2 teaspoons lemon juice
1 tablespoon tomato sauce (ketchup)
½ bird's eye chilli, sliced in half, seeds
   removed and finely chopped
1 tablespoon chopped coriander
   (cilantro) leaves

To make the chilli dressing, place the mayonnaise, sour cream, horseradish cream, lemon juice, tomato sauce, chilli and coriander in a small bowl and mix to combine well. Season to taste with sea salt and freshly ground black pepper.

Finely chop the avocado and squeeze over 1 tablespoon of the lemon juice and season to taste.

Add the prawns and tomato to the chilli dressing and mix until combined. Very finely slice the lettuce leaves and transfer to a bowl. Sprinkle with remaining lemon juice and season lightly with sea salt.

To assemble, divide the lettuce among four 310 ml (10¾ fl oz/1¼ cups) capacity cocktail glasses. Press down gently with a spoon to compact slightly. Scatter over the avocado, then top with the prawn mixture. Serve immediately.

Preparation time: 30 minutes
plus 30 minutes chilling time

Cooking time: 35 minutes

Serves: 6

Tomato-feta tarts with lemon and oregano

125 g (4½ oz) chilled butter, cubed
250 g (9 oz/1⅔ cups) plain (all-purpose)
   flour, sifted, plus extra, for dusting
1 egg, lightly beaten
2 teaspoons finely grated lemon rind
800 g (11 lb 12 oz) grape tomatoes
   (400 g/14 oz each yellow and red)
2 tablespoons olive oil
2 garlic cloves, thinly sliced
1 tablespoon finely chopped oregano
   leaves, plus whole leaves, to serve
1 tablespoon balsamic vinegar
60 g (2¼ oz) feta cheese, crumbled

Preheat the oven to 200°C (400°F/Gas 6). To make pastry, place the butter, flour, egg, lemon rind and a pinch of salt into a food processor bowl. Process for 30 seconds, or until the mixture starts to clump together. If needed, add 1–2 teaspoons of chilled water. Gently knead together on a floured board, then divide mixture into six portions. Alternatively, place the butter, flour and a pinch of salt into a bowl and rub the butter into the flour until mixture resembles coarse breadcrumbs. Mix in the egg and lemon rind until mixture starts to clump together, then gently knead together on a floured board, and divide into 6 portions. Roll each portion into a flattened disc, place on a tray, cover and chill for 30 minutes.

Meanwhile, cut the tomatoes in half and place in a single layer on a baking tray. Drizzle with the oil, then scatter over the garlic and season to taste with sea salt and freshly ground black pepper. Bake for 12–15 minutes or until softened, then remove from oven and reduce oven temperature to 180°C (350°F/Gas 4). Cool tomatoes slightly, then combine in a bowl with oregano and vinegar, and stir gently. Set aside.

Lightly grease six 10 cm (4 inch) tartlet tins with removable bases. Roll out each portion of pastry between 2 sheets of baking paper until about 3 mm (⅛ inch) thick and large enough to line the tins. Press into tins, cutting off any excess pastry. Prick the bases several times with a fork. Line pastry with baking paper and fill with rice or baking beads. Bake for 10 minutes, remove rice or beads, and cook for a further 8–10 minutes or until pastry is light golden. Cool.

To serve, divide tomato filling among pastry cases, sprinkle feta over the top, scatter with oregano leaves and serve immediately.

Mains

Veal and artichoke blanquette • Tarragon, blue eye and white bean bourride • Slow-roast anchovy lamb with pea and mint mash • Veal, eggplant and pasta timballo with cheese sauce • Poulet au pot with sauce agresto • Spicy lamb b'stilla with eggplant jam • Braised beef ribs with turnips, beetroot and horseradish cream • Wine-braised lentils with sausages and fig-balsamic glaze • Pork with potato gratin, roast pear and cider jus • Lamb rump with chickpea tabouleh and chilli-yoghurt sauce • Corned beef with colcannon cakes and prune compote • Indian lamb shanks with spinach, cashew and mint salad • Chicken and green olive braise with sage-almond pesto • Dukkah-crusted fish with cauliflower purée • Harissa lamb chops with apricot-pistachio couscous • Chargrilled Vietnamese chicken with noodle salad • Scotch fillet with anchovy butter and baby beans • Chicken cacciatore with buttery basil mash • Sweet braised pork belly with coconut rice • Roast chicken breast with briam and tzatziki • Fish with asparagus risotto and thyme mascarpone • Lamb shanks with almonds, sherry and brown rice • Veal scaloppine with potato-fennel salad and tuna mayonnaise • Spinach fish rolls with lemon-butter sauce • Root vegetable and goat's cheese tian with hazelnut butter • Roast spatchcock with braised peas and lettuce • Roast pork neck with braised cabbage and apple remoulade • Lamb with bean compote and tomato-basil cream • Braised oxtail with broad beans and parsnip • Roast chicken with bread, lemon and rocket salad • Individual meatloaf Wellingtons with redcurrant-marsala glaze • Grilled swordfish with onion jam and wine potatoes • Chicken drumsticks with pumpkin curry and tamarind chutney • Coconut beef with pineapple and sweet potato salad • Miso and sesame pork with noodle, daikon and seaweed salad

Preparation time: 30 minutes **Cooking time:** 1 hour 30 minutes **Serves:** 4

Veal and artichoke blanquette

1 whole garlic bulb
500 ml (17 fl oz/2 cups) chicken stock
1 leek, white part only, thinly sliced
1 celery stick, roughly chopped
  into 1.5 cm (⅝ inch) pieces
1 large carrot, peeled and roughly
  chopped into 1.5 cm (⅝ inch) pieces
2 thyme sprigs
125 g (4½ oz) small button
  mushrooms, halved
600 g (1 lb 5 oz) veal silverside, cut into
  3 cm (1¼ inch) cubes
1 tablespoon cornflour (cornstarch)
80 ml (2½ fl oz/⅓ cup) cream
3 egg yolks
400 g (14 oz) tin artichoke hearts in
  brine, drained and quartered
1 teaspoon grated lemon rind
1 tablespoon lemon juice
1 small handful parsley, chopped
2 sheets frozen puff pastry, thawed

Preheat the oven to 180°C (350°F/Gas 4). Place the garlic bulb on a small tray and bake for 20 minutes or until soft when tested with a skewer. Set aside to cool.

In a large heavy-based saucepan, bring the stock to the boil, then add the leek, celery, carrot and thyme. Cover, then simmer for 10 minutes. Add the mushrooms and veal cubes. Season with sea salt and freshly ground black pepper. Bring to the boil, then lower heat to simmer and cook, uncovered and stirring occasionally, for 30 minutes or until meat is tender.

In a small bowl, combine cornflour with cream, mixing until smooth, then stir in 2 egg yolks. Pour into the hot veal mixture and stir over low heat until thickened. Do not let mixture boil. Remove thyme and add the artichoke quarters. Cut the roasted garlic in half across the middle. Squeeze the garlic cloves out into the veal mixture. Add lemon rind and juice, and parsley. Cool slightly.

Preheat the oven to 200°C (400°F/Gas 6). Divide the veal mixture among four 375 ml (13 fl oz/1½ cup) capacity ramekins or gratin dishes and place on a baking tray. Cut 4 circles from the pastry sheets to fit over ramekins. Place on top of ramekins, pressing down with a fork to seal the edges. Combine remaining egg yolk with 2 teaspoons of water in a small bowl and brush over pastry. Bake for 25 minutes until pastry is puffed and golden. Serve immediately.

You can leave out the roasted garlic, if you prefer, and substitute the fresh thyme with ½ teaspoon of dried thyme if fresh is unavailable.

Tarragon, blue eye trevalla and white bean bourride

If you're lucky enough to find tarragon in flower, use left-over sprigs to decorate your table. Serve this dish with plenty of crusty bread to mop up the soup.

2 tablespoons olive oil
1 onion, finely chopped
2 leeks, white part only, thinly sliced
2 garlic cloves, finely chopped
3 large tomatoes (about 350 g/12 oz each), peeled and chopped
1 x 6 cm (2½ inch) strip orange zest
Bouquet garni of thyme, parsley, bay leaf and 3 tarragon sprigs
1.5 litres (52 fl oz/6 cups) fish stock or water
2 x 400 g (14 oz) tins white beans, rinsed and drained
750 g (1 lb 10 oz) blue eye trevalla or any other firm white-fleshed fish, cut into 5–8 cm (2–3¼ inches) chunks
1 tablespoon chopped tarragon leaves

Aïoli

3 garlic cloves, crushed
2 teaspoons dijon mustard, at room temperature
1 egg yolk, at room temperature
225 ml (7¾ fl oz) olive oil
2 teaspoons lemon juice

Heat the oil in a large saucepan over medium heat, add the onion, leek and garlic and cook for 5 minutes or until soft. Add the tomato, orange rind, bouquet garni and fish stock. Bring to the boil, reduce heat to low and cook for 30 minutes or until the liquid has reduced by half. Strain the liquid, discarding solids, and return the liquid to the cleaned saucepan. Season to taste with sea salt and freshly ground black pepper. Bring back to the boil, then add the beans and fish, reduce heat to medium–low and cook for 5 minutes or until the fish is just cooked.

Meanwhile to make the aïoli, crush the garlic with a pinch of salt in a mortar and pestle to form a paste. Transfer to a small bowl, add the mustard and egg yolk and whisk to mix well. Then, whisking constantly, add the oil in a slow steady stream until the oil is incorporated and the sauce is very thick. Stir in the lemon juice. Season with extra salt if required.

Divide the soup among large shallow bowls. Spoon some aïoli over each and sprinkle over tarragon leaves. Serve immediately with any remaining aïoli passed separately.

Preparation time: 20 minutes · **Cooking time:** 40 minutes · **Serves:** 6

Preparation time: 35 minutes
plus 20 minutes resting time

Cooking time: 2 hours 20 minutes

Serves: 4–6

Slow-roast anchovy lamb with pea and mint mash

4 garlic cloves, peeled
4 anchovy fillets, drained
2–2.5 kg (4 lb 8 oz–5 lb 8 oz) leg
   of lamb, trimmed of excess fat
80 ml (2½ fl oz/⅓ cup) extra virgin
   olive oil
1 small onion, finely diced
1 rasher of rindless bacon, chopped
460 g (1 lb/3 cups) frozen peas
125 ml (4 fl oz/½ cup) chicken stock
60 ml (2 fl oz/¼ cup) cream
2 teaspoons balsamic vinegar
1 small handful mint, chopped

Preheat the oven to 160°C (315°F/Gas 2–3). Slice the garlic cloves into four pieces lengthways. Chop the anchovies in half. Using a sharp knife make small deep slits all over the lamb, then insert a piece of anchovy or garlic into each slit until the garlic and anchovies are all used.

Place the lamb into a baking tray and rub all over with half of the olive oil. Sprinkle with salt and cook for 1½–2 hours for medium-rare, or until cooked to your liking. Cover loosely with foil and rest in a warm place for 20 minutes.

Meanwhile prepare the peas. Heat the remaining olive oil in a saucepan. Add the onion and bacon and cook, stirring, for 3–4 minutes or until onion has softened. Add the peas and chicken stock, bring to the boil, then cook over medium–high heat for 5 minutes or until the peas are tender and most of the liquid has evaporated. Combine the pea mixture and cream in a food processor and process until a smooth purée forms. Season to taste with sea salt and freshly ground black pepper. Transfer mash to a heatproof bowl, cover and keep warm until ready to serve.

Pour the pan juices from the lamb into a cup. Add balsamic vinegar and water to make quantity up to 250 ml (9 fl oz/1 cup), if necessary. Transfer mixture to a small saucepan and bring to the boil, skimming any fat from the surface as necessary. Cook over medium–high heat for 10 minutes or until liquid is reduced by half. Stir chopped mint into pea mash. Serve slices of lamb with balsamic sauce spooned over and pea mash on the side.

If you prefer the sauce to be thicker, add 2 teaspoons of cornflour (cornstarch) mixed with a little water. Bring to the boil and stir for 1 minute or until thickened.

Veal, eggplant and pasta timballo with cheese sauce

1.2 kg (2 lb 12 oz) medium eggplants
(aubergines) (about 3)
125 ml (4 fl oz/½ cup) olive oil, plus extra,
for greasing

Pasta sauce
2 tablespoons olive oil
500 g (1 lb 2 oz) minced (ground) veal
1 onion, finely chopped
2 garlic cloves, finely chopped
2 x 400 g (14 oz/3½ cups) tins
chopped tomatoes
2 tablespoons tomato paste
(concentrated purée)
1 teaspoon oregano leaves, plus extra
sprigs to serve
250 g (9 oz/2¾ cups) pennette pasta
or other small tubular pasta

Cheese sauce
1½ tablespoons unsalted butter
1 tablespoon plain (all-purpose) flour
250 ml (9 fl oz/1 cup) hot milk
75 g (2¾ oz/¾ cup) grated
parmesan cheese

Cut eggplants widthways into 8 mm (⅜ inch) thick slices. Layer slices in a colander, sprinkling salt over each layer, then stand for 20 minutes or until some of the juices have drained out. Rinse well, then pat dry using paper towels. Preheat the oven to 180°C (350°F/Gas 4). Preheat a chargrill pan to medium. Brush eggplant with oil, then chargrill, in batches, for 2–3 minutes on each side or until tender and slightly charred. Cool.

Meanwhile, to make the pasta sauce, heat half of the oil in a large frying pan over medium–high heat. Add veal and cook, stirring to break up any lumps, for 8–10 minutes or until browned. Transfer to a bowl and set aside. Return pan to the heat. Add remaining oil and onion and cook, stirring often, for 5 minutes or until softened. Return meat to pan and stir in garlic, tomatoes, tomato paste and oregano. Reduce heat and cook for 30–40 minutes or until sauce has reduced and thickened. Remove from heat. Cook pasta in a large saucepan of boiling salted water until al dente, about 10 minutes. Drain well. Add sauce to pasta and mix well.

Grease six 10 cm (4 inch), 250 ml (9 fl oz/ 1 cup) capacity ovenproof ramekins and line with eggplant slices, placing rounded edges in the centre and overhanging edge of dish. You may need to overlap 3 or 4 eggplant slices to completely cover each dish. Divide pasta mixture among ramekins and cover with overhanging eggplant slices, using up any unused slices to cover as necessary. Place ramekins on a baking tray and bake for 25 minutes or until bubbling. Meanwhile, to make the cheese sauce, melt butter in a heavy-based saucepan over medium heat. Stir in flour and cook for 1 minute. Pour in hot milk gradually and whisk until smooth. Reduce heat and cook for 3–5 minutes, until sauce thickens. Remove from heat, stir in parmesan. Season to taste. To serve, carefully invert ramekins onto plates, top with cheese sauce and garnish with oregano.

Preparation time: 30 minutes
plus 20 minutes standing time

Cooking time: 1 hour 30 minutes

Serves: 6

✳ Preparation time: 30 minutes ✳ **Cooking time:** 45 minutes ✳ **Serves:** 4

Poulet au pot with sauce agresto

1.5 kg (3 lb 5 oz) chicken
1 whole garlic bulb, top cut off
2 bay leaves
4 thyme sprigs
1 teaspoon peppercorns
2 leeks, trimmed, cleaned and
   sliced thickly
1 bunch baby carrots (about 350 g/12 oz),
   cleaned and peeled
400 g (14 oz) desiree potatoes
   (about 2), peeled and cut into
   3 cm (1¼ inch) pieces
400 g (14 oz) baby turnips (about
   1 bunch), peeled and stalks trimmed
400 g (14 oz) frozen broad (fava) beans,
   cooked, cooled and peeled

Sauce agresto

60 g (2¼ oz/⅓ cup) blanched almonds
30 g (1 oz/¼ cup) walnuts
1 garlic clove
2 large handfuls parsley
1 small handful basil
125 ml (4 fl oz/½ cup) olive oil
125 ml (4 fl oz/½ cup) verjuice or
   lemon juice

For the sauce agresto, preheat the oven to 200°C (400°F/Gas 6). Roast the almonds and walnuts on separate baking trays for about 5 minutes or until golden. Rub walnuts in a clean tea towel to remove the skins, then cool. Combine the nuts, garlic, herbs and ½ teaspoon salt in a food processor with 2 tablespoons of the olive oil and process until a coarse paste forms. With the motor running, slowly add the verjuice and remaining oil and process until mixture is smooth. Transfer to a clean bowl and set aside

Sprinkle the chicken with 1 teaspoon sea salt and rub into the skin, then place in a large saucepan with the garlic, bay leaves, thyme and peppercorns. Add enough cold water to cover the chicken, then bring to the boil over medium heat, skimming off any scum that forms. Reduce the heat to low and cook chicken for 15 minutes. Add all vegetables except the broad beans to the pot and continue to cook for 20–25 minutes or until the vegetables are tender and the juices run clear when the chicken is pierced between the thigh and body. Add the peeled broad beans and cook for 1 minute or until heated through. Remove the chicken from the liquid and cool for 6 minutes. Tear the meat from the carcass in large chunks and divide among 4 deep bowls. Add the vegetables and some of the broth and serve topped with a tablespoon of sauce agresto.

Use any green vegetable you like instead of broad beans – peas, sugar snaps, green beans, snow peas (mangetouts) or blanched brussels sprouts are all good choices. You will need to adjust the cooking time accordingly.

Spicy lamb b'stilla with eggplant jam

600 g (1 lb 5 oz) lamb shoulder, trimmed
and cut into 4 cm (1½ inch) cubes
2 tablespoons plain (all-purpose) flour
2 tablespoons olive oil, plus extra, for
greasing and brushing
2 small onions, finely chopped
2 carrots, peeled and chopped
2 garlic cloves, crushed
1 tablespoon ginger, finely grated
2 teaspoons ground cinnamon
2 teaspoons ground cumin
1 teaspoon ground coriander
500 ml (17 fl oz/2 cups) beef stock
75 g (2¾ oz/½ cup) currants
1 large handful coriander (cilantro)
leaves, chopped
60 g (2¼ oz/½ cup) icing (confectioner's)
sugar, plus extra for dusting
2 tablespoons flaked almonds
7 filo pastry sheets

Eggplant jam

2 tablespoons olive oil, plus extra,
for brushing
900 g (2 lb) medium eggplants
(aubergines) (about 2), cut into
3 cm (1¼ inch) pieces
1 garlic clove, crushed
½ teaspoon ground cinnamon
1 teaspoon sweet paprika
1 teaspoon cayenne pepper
110 g (3¾ oz/½ cup) caster
(superfine) sugar
finely grated rind and juice of 1 lemon
1 small handful coriander (cilantro)
leaves, chopped

To make the eggplant jam, heat oil in a heavy-based saucepan over medium heat. Add eggplant and cook, stirring regularly, for 10 minutes or until soft. Add garlic and spices and cook, stirring constantly, for 1 minute, then add sugar, lemon rind and 60 ml (2 fl oz/¼ cup) water. Reduce heat to low and cook for 15 minutes, stirring constantly, until liquid has been absorbed. Stir in lemon juice and coriander. Season with sea salt and freshly ground black pepper. Remove from heat and cool.

Dust lamb lightly in flour, shaking off excess. Heat oil in a large heavy-based saucepan over medium heat. Add half of the lamb and cook for 5 minutes, turning often, or until browned all over. Remove to a plate and repeat with remaining lamb. Add onion and carrot to the pan and cook for 2 minutes, stirring, or until onion is soft, then add garlic, ginger and spices, stirring constantly. Return lamb to pan with stock and currants. Bring to the boil, then reduce heat and simmer, covered, for 45 minutes or until meat is tender. Uncover and simmer for 20 minutes, or until most of the liquid has evaporated and the meat is falling apart. Cool, then stir in coriander.

Preheat the oven to 200°C (400°F/Gas 6). Combine icing sugar and almonds in a bowl. Grease six 150 ml (5 fl oz) capacity muffin holes with oil. Lay 1 sheet of pastry on a work surface, brush with oil, top with another pastry sheet, brush with oil and repeat with 2 more sheets. Using a sharp knife, cut pastry into six 15 x 13 cm (6 x 5 inches) rectangles and use to line muffin holes. Divide half the icing sugar mixture among holes. Top with lamb mixture. Layer remaining pastry sheets, brushing each sheet lightly with oil. Using a sharp knife, cut pastry rounds large enough to cover meat mixture, tucking in any excess pastry to enclose. Brush tops with oil, then sprinkle with remaining sugar mixture. Bake for 20 minutes, or until pastry is crisp. Dust with icing sugar and serve with eggplant jam.

Preparation time: 30 minutes   **Cooking time:** 2 hours   **Serves:** 6

✳ **Preparation time:** 30 minutes ✳ **Cooking time:** 4 hours 30 minutes ✳ **Serves:** 6

Braised beef ribs with turnips, beetroot and horseradish cream

80 ml (2½ fl oz/⅓ cup) vegetable oil
2 celery sticks, trimmed and
  finely chopped
1 onion, finely chopped
1 leek, white part only, thinly sliced
1 carrot, finely chopped
2 garlic cloves, chopped
2 fresh bay leaves
2 thyme sprigs
75 g (2¾ oz/½ cup) plain
  (all-purpose) flour
2 kg (4 lb 8 oz) beef ribs in 3 cm (1¼ inch)
  pieces, cut between the bones (ask your
  butcher to do this for you)
400 g (14 oz/about 10) baby
  beetroot (beets)
400 g (14 oz) baby turnips (about 24)
250 ml (9 fl oz/1 cup) red wine
875 ml (30 fl oz/3½ cups) beef stock
125 g (4½ oz/½ cup) sour cream
2 tablespoons horseradish cream,
  or to taste
chopped flat-leaf (Italian) parsley, to serve

Preheat the oven to 160°C (315°F/Gas 2-3).

Heat 1 tablespoon of the oil in a very large, heavy-based flameproof casserole dish. Add the chopped vegetables and garlic, and cook, stirring, for 5 minutes or until softened. Stir in the herbs, then remove the casserole dish from heat.

Place flour in a large bowl and season with sea salt and freshly ground black pepper. Add beef ribs, toss to coat in flour and shake off any excess.

Heat half the remaining vegetable oil in a large, heavy-based frying pan over medium heat, add half the ribs and cook for 5 minutes, turning often, or until golden all over. Remove browned ribs to the casserole dish, then repeat process with remaining oil and ribs. Peel the baby beetroot and turnips and add to casserole with wine and stock. Season to taste, then bring mixture slowly to a gentle boil. Cover tightly, transfer to the oven and cook for 4 hours or until beef is starting to fall off the bone and beetroot is tender.

Remove the meat and vegetables from the casserole dish and cover to keep warm. Simmer the cooking liquid for 20 minutes or until reduced and thickened slightly, skimming to remove excess fat. While the liquid is reducing, combine the sour cream and horseradish in a small bowl, stirring to mix well. Season to taste.

Return the meat and vegetables to the casserole dish and heat gently to warm through. Serve sprinkled with chopped parsley, with horseradish cream on the side.

Wine-braised lentils with sausages and fig-balsamic glaze

12 thin Italian-style pork sausages
  (about 90 g/3¼ oz each)
60 ml (2 fl oz/¼ cup) balsamic vinegar
125 g (4½ oz) purchased fig jam

Wine-braised lentils

2 tablespoons olive oil
1 large onion, finely chopped
65 g (2¼ oz) prosciutto (about
  4 thin slices), chopped
1 carrot, finely diced
1 celery stick, finely diced
1 bay leaf
2 garlic cloves, crushed
250 ml (9 fl oz/1 cup) white wine
280 g (10 oz/1½ cups) brown lentils
1 handful flat-leaf (Italian) parsley,
  chopped, plus 2 tablespoons extra,
  to serve

To make the wine-braised lentils, heat 1½ tablespoons of the oil in a heavy-based saucepan over medium heat. Add onion and cook for 5 minutes or until softened. Add prosciutto, carrot and celery and cook for 5 minutes or until vegetables are soft. Add bay leaf, garlic and wine, cook for 1 minute, then add lentils and enough water to just cover. Bring to the boil, reduce heat to medium–low, then partially cover with a lid. Cook for 45 minutes or until lentils are tender and liquid has been absorbed. Stir in parsley and season to taste with sea salt and freshly ground black pepper.

Meanwhile, heat the remaining oil in a large frying pan over a medium–high heat. Cook sausages, turning, for 10–12 minutes until golden and cooked through. Combine balsamic vinegar, jam and 1 tablespoon of water in a bowl, then add mixture to sausages in pan and bring to a simmer. Cook for 1–2 minutes, turning the sausages often to coat in the glaze. Remove from the heat.

To serve, divide the lentils among the plates, then top each with 2 sausages. Spoon any remaining glaze over the sausages, then serve immediately sprinkled with parsley.

Preparation time: 15 minutes   **Cooking time:** 1 hour   **Serves:** 6

Preparation time: 35 minutes   **Cooking time:** 1 hour 35 minutes   **Serves:** 6

Pork with potato gratin, roast pear and cider jus

825 g (1 lb 13 oz) large potatoes (about 4)
300 ml (10½ fl oz) cream
3 tablespoons dijon mustard
1 tablespoon chopped rosemary
1.4 kg (3 lb 2 oz) boned, rolled pork leg,
  skin scored (ask your butcher to do this)
2 tablespoons vegetable oil
3 beurre bosc pears
30 g (1 oz) butter, melted
1 tablespoon caster (superfine) sugar
125 ml (4 fl oz/½ cup) cider
125 ml (4 fl oz/½ cup) chicken stock

Preheat the oven to 200°C (400°F/Gas 6). While oven is heating, grease a 20 cm (8 inch) square cake tin or similar-sized square baking dish. Peel the potatoes and slice thinly, using either a mandolin, food processor or by hand. In a stainless-steel bowl, whisk together 250 ml (9 fl oz/1 cup) of the cream, 2 tablespoons of the mustard, rosemary and sea salt to taste. Place slices of potato into the tin in neat layers, until all potato is used, seasoning potatoes lightly with sea salt and freshly ground black pepper as you go. Pour cream mixture over, cover and set aside.

Place the pork in a large flameproof roasting pan and rub all over with the vegetable oil. Sprinkle a generous amount of sea salt (about 1 tablespoon) over the pork skin, then roast for 20 minutes. Meanwhile halve the pears lengthways and remove the cores. Brush the pears with melted butter and sprinkle with the caster sugar. When the pork has roasted for 20 minutes, reduce the heat to 180°C (350°F/Gas 4) and add pears to the dish, cut side down. Place the potato gratin in the oven. Cook pork, pears and potatoes for 50 minutes or until pork is just cooked; turn pears over halfway through. Remove pork to a large plate, cover loosely with foil and stand in a warm place; cook gratin and pears for another 10 minutes or until tender.

Transfer the pears to the pork plate and turn oven off; gratin will keep warm in cooling oven while you make the sauce. Carefully skim excess fat from pan, then place the roasting pan over medium heat on the stove top. Add cider, stock and remaining mustard, bring to a gentle boil and cook, stirring to remove any sediment stuck to the base of the pan, for 10 minutes or until liquid is reduced by half. Add the remaining cream and simmer for 5 minutes or until reduced and slightly thickened. Serve the pork, sliced, with a slice of gratin, pear and sauce.

Lamb rump with chickpea tabouleh and chilli-yoghurt sauce

700 g (1 lb 9 oz) lamb rump steaks
1 tablespoon olive oil
1 teaspoon ground cumin
90 g (3¼ oz/½ cup) fine burghul
 (cracked wheat)
1 x 400 g (14 oz) tin chickpeas
 (garbanzo beans), drained well
2 tomatoes (about 150 g/5½ oz each),
 cut into 2 cm (¾ inch) pieces
2 spring onions (scallions), trimmed
 and finely sliced
1 handful mint, roughly chopped
1 teaspoon finely grated lemon rind
50 ml (1¾ fl oz) lemon juice
1 large handful flat-leaf (Italian) parsley,
 roughly chopped
1 large handful coriander (cilantro)
 leaves, roughly chopped

Chilli-yoghurt sauce
125 g (4½ oz/½ cup) natural yoghurt
1 long green chilli, or to taste, seeded
 and finely chopped
1 tablespoon mint sauce
1 large handful mint, chopped
1 large handful coriander (cilantro)
 leaves, chopped

Preheat the oven to 200°C (400°F/Gas 6).

Brush the steaks with half of the olive oil, then sprinkle with ground cumin and season with sea salt and freshly ground black pepper to taste. Heat a chargrill pan over medium heat. Add the lamb steaks and cook for 2 minutes each side for medium-rare or until cooked to your liking. Remove from heat and place on a plate, loosely cover with foil, then rest in a warm place.

Meanwhile, place burghul in a bowl. Pour over 375 ml (13 fl oz/1½ cups) boiling water, cover and stand for 15 minutes or until tender. Drain well. Stir in the chickpeas, tomato, spring onion, mint, lemon rind and juice, parsley, coriander and remaining olive oil. Season to taste with sea salt and freshly ground black pepper.

To make the chilli-yoghurt sauce, in a bowl combine yoghurt, chilli, mint sauce, mint and coriander until smooth.

Divide the chickpea tabouleh among plates. Slice lamb steaks thickly on the diagonal, then divide lamb among plates, top with yoghurt sauce and serve immediately.

Preparation time: 20 minutes **Cooking time:** 5 minutes **Serves:** 4

Preparation time: 30 minutes   **Cooking time:** 1 hour 50 minutes   **Serves:** 6

Corned beef with colcannon cakes and prune compote

1.4 kg (3 lb 2 oz) piece corned
  beef silverside
2 carrots, peeled and cut into
  2 cm (¾ inch) pieces
1 onion, coarsely chopped
1 tablespoon malt vinegar
500 g (1 lb 2 oz) waxy potatoes,
  such as desiree
20 g (¾ oz) butter
1 leek, white part only, thinly sliced
300 g (10½ oz/4 cups) finely shredded
  green cabbage (about ¼ cabbage)
1 bunch English spinach, stems removed,
  thinly sliced
1 egg, lightly beaten
75 g (2¾ oz/½ cup) plain
  (all-purpose) flour
olive oil, for shallow frying
watercress sprigs, to serve (optional)

Prune compote
2 firm ripe William pears, peeled, cored
  and chopped into 1 cm (½ inch) cubes
110 g (3¾ oz/½ cup) pitted prunes, halved
125 ml (4 fl oz/½ cup) red wine
125 ml (4 fl oz/½ cup) chicken stock
1 pinch ground allspice

To make the prune compote, combine all the ingredients in a small saucepan, bring to the boil, then reduce heat to low and cook for 20 minutes or until liquid has reduced and mixture is thick and has a jam-like consistency. Cool.

Place silverside in a large saucepan, then add carrot, onion and vinegar. Cover with cold water, bring to the boil, then reduce the heat to a simmer. Cook the meat, covered, over low heat for 1½ hours or until meat is cooked through. Remove corned beef from the cooking liquid, draining well, then transfer to a warmed plate and cover with foil to keep warm.

Meanwhile place potatoes in a saucepan of salted cold water, bring to the boil and cook for 15–20 minutes or until tender. Drain and mash with half of the butter until smooth.

Heat the remaining butter in a frying pan over low heat. Add the leek and cabbage and cook, stirring, for 5 minutes or until vegetables are starting to soften. Add the spinach and cook for another minute or until wilted. Combine the cabbage mixture and egg with the potato in a large bowl, season to taste with sea salt and freshly ground black pepper, then cool. Divide the mixture into 6 even-sized portions, then form each into a round cake about 6 cm (2½ inches) across.

Dust the cakes in flour, shaking off excess. Heat the oil in a large frying pan over medium heat, add the cakes and cook for 3 minutes each side, or until golden. Serve slices of corned beef topped with prune compote, with colcannon cakes and watercress, if using, on the side.

Indian lamb shanks with spinach, cashew and mint salad

1 small onion, chopped
3 garlic cloves
5 cm (2 inch) piece ginger, peeled
  and sliced
1 teaspoon ground cumin
1 teaspoon ground garam masala
300 g (10½ oz/1¼ cups) natural yoghurt
90 g (3¼ oz/⅓ cup) tomato paste
  (concentrated purée)
4 x 300 g (10½ oz) French-trimmed
  lamb shanks

Spinach salad

1 tablespoon vegetable oil
2 teaspoons brown mustard seeds
½ red onion, very finely sliced
1 small handful mint, torn
4 large handfuls baby spinach leaves
125 g (4½ oz) cherry tomatoes
  (½ punnet), quartered
2 tablespoons lime juice
1 tablespoon extra virgin olive oil
80 g (2¾ oz/½ cup) roasted
  unsalted cashews
naan bread, to serve

Combine the onion, garlic, ginger, spices and ½ teaspoon sea salt in a food processor and process until a coarse paste forms. Add the yoghurt and tomato paste, then pulse to combine well. Using the point of a small, sharp knife, pierce each shank 3–4 times. Combine the meat and yoghurt paste in a ceramic dish, turning to coat meat well, then cover and refrigerate for 3 hours or overnight.

Transfer the meat and marinade to a heavy-based saucepan large enough to fit shanks in a single layer. Pour in 100 ml (3½ fl oz) of water. Bring to the boil, cover with the lid, reduce heat to low and cook for 1 hour or until tender, turning halfway through cooking time and adding a little extra water if the meat begins to catch on the base of the pan.

Meanwhile, to make the spinach salad, heat vegetable oil in a small frying pan over medium heat. Add the mustard seeds and cook for 30 seconds or until they begin to pop. Pour the oil and seeds over the onion in a bowl and set aside to cool. Add the mint, spinach and tomatoes to the bowl. Whisk together the lime juice and olive oil, pour over and toss gently to coat well. Scatter with cashews.

Divide the lamb shanks and salad among serving plates and serve with plenty of naan bread on the side to mop up the juices.

Preparation time: 30 minutes
plus 3 hours marinating time

Cooking time: 1 hour

Serves: 4

Preparation time: 20 minutes   **Cooking time:** 50 minutes   **Serves:** 4–6

Chicken and green olive braise with sage-almond pesto

1.25 kg (2 lb 12 oz) large chicken thighs, with skin and bone (about 6)
2 tablespoons olive oil
1 large onion, chopped
2 garlic cloves, crushed
185 ml (6 fl oz/¾ cup) chicken stock
125 ml (4 fl oz/½ cup) white wine
1 tablespoon chopped sage
2 strips lemon zest
500 g (1 lb 2 oz) kipfler (fingerling) or other waxy potatoes, peeled and cut into 3 cm (1¼ inch) chunks
20 pitted green olives

Sage-almond pesto
80 g (2¾ oz/½ cup) blanched almonds, lightly toasted and chopped
1 large handful flat-leaf (Italian) parsley
1 tablespoon chopped sage
1 teaspoon finely grated lemon rind
1 small garlic clove, crushed
60 ml (2 fl oz/¼ cup) olive oil
45 g (1¾ oz/½ cup) grated pecorino cheese

To make the sage-almond pesto, combine all the ingredients in a food processor and process until a coarse paste forms, adding a little extra olive oil if necessary. Season to taste with sea salt and freshly ground black pepper, then transfer to a bowl. Cover the surface with plastic wrap to prevent discolouration and set aside until needed.

Remove excess fat from the chicken. Using a large sharp knife, trim thighs into a neat shape, then season to taste. Heat olive oil in a large frying pan. Add half of the chicken and cook over medium heat for about 2 minutes on each side until golden brown. Remove from the pan and repeat with remaining chicken.

Pour excess oil from the pan leaving about 2 tablespoons in pan, then add the onion and cook, stirring, over medium heat for 5 minutes or until soft but not brown. Add the garlic and cook 1 minute longer. Add the stock, wine, sage and lemon zest, and season to taste. Bring to the boil, then add the potatoes and olives. Reduce heat to low, add the chicken, then cover the pan with foil and a tight-fitting lid. Cook for 35–40 minutes or until the chicken and potatoes are cooked.

Divide the chicken, vegetables and cooking liquid among deep plates, top with the pesto and serve immediately.

Dukkah-crusted fish with cauliflower purée

60 ml (2 fl oz/¼ cup) extra virgin olive oil
40 g (1½ oz) butter
1 small onion, finely chopped
1 garlic clove, finely chopped
500 g (1 lb 2 oz) cauliflower (about
   1 small one), trimmed and cut into florets
250 ml (9 fl oz/1 cup) chicken stock
50 ml (1¾ fl oz) lemon juice
2 eggs
50 ml (1¾ fl oz) milk
4 x 200 g (7 oz) basa, or other white
   fish, fillets
100 g (3½ oz/¾ cup) dukkah
60 ml (2 fl oz/¼ cup) vegetable oil
rocket (arugula) and lemon cheeks,
   to serve

Preheat the oven to 160°C (315°F/Gas 2–3). Heat olive oil and butter in a saucepan over medium–low heat. Add the onion and garlic and cook for 2–3 minutes or until softened. Add the chopped cauliflower and chicken stock, bring to the boil, then reduce heat to low. Cook, stirring occasionally, for 15 minutes or until most of the liquid has evaporated and the cauliflower is very tender; do not allow cauliflower to brown. Transfer mixture to a food processor, add lemon juice and process until a smooth purée forms. Season to taste with sea salt and freshly ground black pepper. Transfer to a heatproof bowl, cover tightly with foil and keep warm in the oven.

Break the eggs into a small bowl and whisk together with the milk.

Place the dukkah into another small bowl. Dip each piece of fish into the egg mix, drain off excess egg, then coat in the dukkah, pressing dukkah onto fish to coat evenly.

Reduce the oven temperature to 150°C (300°F/Gas 2).

Heat the vegetable oil in a large frying pan over medium heat. Add the fish, in batches, and cook for 2–3 minutes on each side or until golden and cooked through. Transfer the cooked fish to the oven to keep warm while cooking the remaining fish.

Spoon cauliflower purée onto warmed plates and top each with a piece of fish. Serve immediately with lemon cheeks and rocket on the side.

Preparation time: 30 minutes   **Cooking time:** 25 minutes   **Serves:** 4

Preparation time: 20 minutes   **Cooking time:** 20 minutes   **Serves:** 4

Harissa lamb chops with apricot-pistachio couscous

1 x 425 g (15 oz) tin apricot halves in juice
finely grated rind and juice of 1 orange
30 g (1 oz) butter
2 tablespoons olive oil
50 g (1¾ oz/⅓ cup) currants
300 g (10½ oz/1½ cups) instant couscous
8 (about 800 g/1 lb 12 oz) lamb loin chops
50 g (1¾ oz/⅓ cup) pistachios, chopped
1 large handful coriander (cilantro)
   leaves, chopped
2 baby cos (romaine) lettuces, washed and
   leaves separated, to serve (optional)
lemon wedges, to serve (optional)

Harissa

2 red capsicums (peppers)
2 teaspoons ground cumin
2 teaspoons ground coriander
1 tablespoon lemon juice, or to taste
2 garlic cloves, chopped
1 teaspoon chilli flakes, or to taste
125 ml (4 fl oz/½ cup) extra virgin olive oil

To make the harissa, preheat the oven grill (broiler) to high. Place whole capsicums on a baking tray and place under the grill, about 2 cm (¾ inch) from heat source. Grill capsicums, turning often, for 5–6 minutes or until skin is black and blistered all over. Place capsicums in a plastic bag and seal. When cool enough to handle, remove blistered skin, stem and seeds; try not to run capsicum under water as you do this or you will loose flavour. Chop capsicum flesh coarsely, then combine in a food processor with all the ingredients except the olive oil. Process until a coarse paste forms, then add olive oil and process until smooth. Season to taste with sea salt and freshly ground black pepper and add a little more lemon juice if necessary.

Preheat the oven to 120°C (235°F/Gas ½). Drain apricots well, reserving the juice. Combine the reserved juice, orange rind and juice, then add enough water to make quantity up to 375 ml (13 fl oz/1½ cups). Combine mixture in a saucepan with the butter and 1 tablespoon of the oil and bring just to the boil.

Place the currants and couscous in a large bowl, then pour the hot liquid over the top. Stir to combine, then cover the bowl with plastic wrap and stand for 5 minutes or until liquid is absorbed. Fluff with a fork.

Heat the remaining oil in a frying pan, add lamb chops and cook over medium heat for 3 minutes on each side or until golden and just cooked through. Transfer to a plate, cover with foil then place in the oven to keep warm. Meanwhile chop the apricots and add to the couscous with the pistachios and coriander. Season to taste.

Divide the couscous evenly among plates. Place 2 lamb chops on each plate and top with harissa. Serve with cos lettuce leaves and lemon wedges, if using.

Chargrilled Vietnamese chicken with noodle salad

60 ml (2 fl oz/¼ cup) lime juice
60 ml (2 fl oz/¼ cup) fish sauce
1 tablespoon caster (superfine) sugar
1 tablespoon sweet chilli sauce
1 small red onion, thinly sliced
800 g (1 lb 12 oz) chicken thigh
   fillets, trimmed
1 tablespoon peanut oil
80 g (2¾ oz/½ cup) roasted peanuts

Noodle salad
200 g (7 oz) flat, thin rice noodles
1 carrot, peeled and cut into thin
   matchsticks
1 telegraph (long) cucumber, seeded
   and thinly sliced
65 g (2½ oz/¾ cup) bean sprouts
50 g (1¾ oz/1 cup) shredded
   Chinese cabbage
1 small handful mint
1 small handful coriander (cilantro) leaves
1 small handful basil
1 large red chilli, seeded and thinly sliced

Place the lime juice, fish sauce, caster sugar, sweet chilli and red onion in a small bowl and stir until well combined. Set aside.

Place the chicken and oil in a bowl, season to taste with sea salt and freshly ground black pepper and toss to combine well. Heat a large chargrill pan over medium heat. Cook the chicken for 5 minutes on each side or until cooked through. Remove to a warmed plate, cover loosely with foil and stand in a warm place for 5 minutes. Slice thinly on the diagonal.

To make the noodle salad, cook the noodles in boiling water for 3 minutes or according to packet instructions until tender, then drain well. Stand under cold running water until cool, then drain well. Place the noodles in a large bowl with the carrot, cucumber, bean sprouts, cabbage, herbs and chilli and toss to combine well.

Add the chicken and prepared dressing to the noodle salad and gently toss to combine. Divide among the serving plates, sprinkle with the peanuts and serve.

Preparation time: 15 minutes   **Cooking time:** 15 minutes   **Serves:** 6

Preparation time: 20 minutes
plus 1 hour chilling time

Cooking time: 10 minutes

Serves: 4

Scotch fillet with anchovy butter and baby beans

4 x 175 g (6 oz) Scotch fillet steaks
Olive oil, for brushing steaks
150 g (5½ oz) baby butterbeans
  (lima beans), trimmed
150 g (5½ oz) baby green beans

Anchovy butter
4 anchovy fillets
75 g (2¾ oz) unsalted butter, softened
1 teaspoon finely chopped rosemary
1 garlic clove, crushed
1 teaspoon finely grated lemon
  rind (optional)

For the anchovy butter, chop the anchovy fillets very finely until you have a mashed consistency. Combine the butter, anchovies, rosemary, garlic and lemon, if using, in a small bowl. Mix well with a fork and season with freshly ground black pepper. Spoon the butter along the middle of a 30 x 15 cm (12 x 6 inch) piece of baking paper. Form into a log shape, about 3 cm (1¼ inches) in diameter, then roll paper around the butter to enclose completely. Carefully transfer the butter to a tray and refrigerate for at least 1 hour or until set. Anchovy butter can be made up to 1 week in advance.

Preheat a chargrill plate or large, heavy-based frying pan over a high heat until pan is very hot. Lightly oil the steaks on each side and season with sea salt and freshly ground black pepper. Cook the steaks for 3–4 minutes each side for medium-rare, or until cooked to your liking. Transfer to a plate and cover loosely with foil.

Meanwhile, cook the beans in a large saucepan of boiling salted water for 5–7 minutes until just tender. Drain well. Cut the anchovy butter into 1 cm (½ inch) thick slices. Divide the beans and steaks among serving plates, top steaks with discs of butter and serve immediately.

Chicken cacciatore with buttery basil mash

2 tablespoons olive oil
1.5 kg (3 lb 5 oz) chicken, cut into
  8 pieces (ask your butcher to do this)
1 onion, sliced
3 anchovy fillets, chopped
2 garlic cloves, crushed
125 ml (4 fl oz/½ cup) white wine
125 ml (4 fl oz/½ cup) chicken stock
1 tablespoon tomato paste
  (concentrated purée)
1 x 400 g (14 oz) tin chopped tomatoes
1 teaspoon brown sugar
1 large handful flat-leaf (Italian)
  parsley, torn

Basil mash
800 g (1 lb 12 oz) waxy potatoes such as
  desiree (about 6), peeled and chopped
50 g (1¾ oz) unsalted butter, chopped
1 small handful basil, roughly chopped

Preheat the oven to 180°C (350°F/Gas 4). Heat the oil in a large ovenproof saucepan. Add the chicken, in batches, and cook over medium–high heat for 4–5 minutes on each side or until golden. Remove the chicken from the pan. Reduce heat to medium, add the onion and anchovies and cook, stirring, for 1 minute or until onion has softened. Add the garlic and cook for 1 minute or until aromatic. Add the wine, stirring to remove any sediment on the base of the pan, then bring to the boil over high heat. Add the chicken, stock, tomato paste, chopped tomatoes and sugar and return to the boil. Reduce heat to medium and cook for 4–5 minutes. Cover, transfer to the oven and cook for 1 hour or until chicken is tender.

Meanwhile, to make the basil mash, cook the potatoes in boiling salted water until tender. Drain the potatoes well, then return to the pan, add the butter and mash with a potato masher until smooth. Stir in the basil and season to taste with sea salt and freshly ground black pepper.

Serve the chicken with the basil mash and sprinkle with parsley.

Preparation time: 20 minutes ✳ **Cooking time:** 1 hour 30 minutes ✳ **Serves:** 4

Preparation time: 20 minutes
plus 1 hour chilling time

Cooking time: 1 hour 50 minutes

Serves: 4

Sweet braised pork belly with coconut rice

1 kg (2 lb 4 oz) piece pork belly, skin on
and boned (ask your butcher to do this)
2 tablespoons honey
1½ teaspoons Chinese five-spice powder
2 tablespoons oil
5 garlic cloves, thinly sliced
1.5 cm (⅝ inch) piece ginger, sliced
2 spring onions (scallions), trimmed and
chopped, plus extra, diagonally sliced,
to serve
2 star anise
60 ml (2 fl oz/¼ cup) soy sauce
100 g (3½ oz/¾ cup) shaved palm
sugar (jaggery)
¼ teaspoon ground white pepper
250 ml (9 fl oz/1 cup) chicken stock

Coconut rice
200 g (7 oz/1 cup) long-grain or
jasmine rice
125 ml (4 fl oz/½ cup) coconut cream

Cut the pork in half lengthways and slice each half into eight pieces. Combine the honey, five-spice powder and 1 tablespoon of warm water in a large bowl and stir to combine well. Place the meat in a bowl and rub the honey mixture all over the meat. Cover the bowl with plastic wrap and refrigerate for 1 hour.

Heat the oil in a large saucepan over medium–high heat, add the pork pieces and cook, turning, for 4–5 minutes or until the skin is slightly charred and the meat is brown. Take care when cooking as the skin will spit. Drain off any excess fat.

Add the garlic, ginger and spring onions and stir-fry for about 1 minute or until fragrant. Add the star anise, soy sauce, palm sugar, white pepper, stock and 250 ml (9 fl oz/1 cup) water. Bring the mixture just to the boil, then reduce heat to low, cover pan and cook meat gently for 1½ hours, turning occasionally or until the meat is very tender. Remove the meat to a bowl and skim excess fat from surface of cooking liquid. Remove the ginger and star anise, then bring liquid to the boil and cook for 10–15 minutes or until reduced and thickened slightly. Return the meat to the liquid, cover and heat through.

Meanwhile, to make the coconut rice, rinse the rice under cold water until the water runs almost clear. Drain well, then combine in a saucepan with the coconut cream and 250 ml (9 fl oz/1 cup) water. Bring to the boil, then reduce heat to medium–low, cover tightly and cook for 10–12 minutes or until most of the liquid is absorbed. Remove from heat and stand the rice for 10 minutes or until tender. Divide the rice among the serving plates, add the pork pieces, spoon over the reduced cooking juices and serve topped with spring onion.

Roast chicken breast with briam and tzatziki

4 small vine-ripened tomatoes, with
  stem attached
80 ml (2½ fl oz/⅓ cup) olive oil
4 x 200 g (7 oz) chicken breast fillets,
  with skin on
1 rosemary sprig
1 garlic clove, peeled and lightly crushed
250 ml (9 fl oz/1 cup) purchased tzatziki,
  to serve

Briam
350 g (12 oz) eggplant (aubergine), cut
  into 2 cm (¾ inch) cubes
300 g (10½ oz) medium zucchini
  (courgettes) (about 2), cut into
  2 cm (¾ inch) pieces
300 g (10½ oz) medium potatoes
  (about 2), peeled and cut into
  2 cm (¾ inch) pieces
1 medium red capsicum (pepper), seeded
  and cut into 2 cm (¾ inch) pieces
600 g (1 lb 5 oz) tomatoes (about 3), cut
  into chunks
1 large red onion, halved and thinly sliced
4 garlic cloves, crushed
1 tablespoon dried oregano
2 teaspoons ground cumin
2 bay leaves
125 ml (4 fl oz/½ cup) chicken stock
  or water
125 ml (4 fl oz/½ cup) olive oil
1 handful flat-leaf (Italian)
  parsley, chopped

For the briam, preheat the oven to 180°C (350°F/ Gas 4). Place all the vegetables, garlic, oregano, cumin and bay leaves in a large bowl and combine thoroughly. Add stock or water and oil and toss again. Put in a large roasting pan and shake to settle. Bake covered with foil for 30 minutes, then uncover and bake for 45 minutes–1 hour or until golden and tender, tossing vegetables occasionally. Stir through parsley and season with sea salt and freshly ground black pepper.

Meanwhile, place the vine-ripened tomatoes on a baking paper-lined baking tray and drizzle with 1 tablespoon of the olive oil. Bake for 10–15 minutes until just soft but not collapsed.

Meanwhile, heat the remaining olive oil in a large, ovenproof frying pan over medium–high heat. Add the chicken breasts to the pan, skin side down, and cook for 2–3 minutes or until light golden. Turn chicken over, season to taste, then add the rosemary, garlic and 125 ml (4 fl oz/½ cup) water. Working quickly, remove from the heat, cover the pan tightly with foil, transfer to the oven and cook for 15 minutes or until the chicken is almost cooked through. Stand chicken, covered, for 5 minutes to rest.

To serve, divide the briam among the serving plates. Remove the chicken from the cooking liquid and drain well. Arrange the chicken next to the briam, spoon over some tzatziki and place a roast tomato on the side. Serve immediately with remaining tzatziki served separately.

Preparation time: 25 minutes   **Cooking time:** 1 hour 30 minutes   **Serves:** 4

Preparation time: 20 minutes   **Cooking time:** 40 minutes   **Serves:** 6

Fish with asparagus risotto and thyme mascarpone

80 ml (2½ fl oz/⅓ cup) olive oil

1 leek, white part only, thinly sliced

100 g (3½ oz) piece pancetta, chopped

330 g (11¾ oz/1½ cups) arborio or other risotto rice

125 ml (4 fl oz/½ cup) white wine

1.25 litres (44 fl oz/5 cups) fish or chicken stock, simmering

12–16 spears of asparagus (about 2 bunches), trimmed and cut into 3 cm (1¼ inch) pieces

20 g (¾ oz) butter, chopped

25 g (1 oz/¼ cup) grated parmesan cheese

3 teaspoons finely grated lemon rind

4 x 120 g (4¼ oz) basa, or other white fish fillets

75 g (2¾ oz/½ cup) polenta

60 g (2¼ oz/¼ cup) mascarpone cheese

1 tablespoon thyme leaves, lightly bruised

Heat half the oil in a large saucepan over medium heat, add the leek and pancetta. Cook, stirring, for 5 minutes or until softened, then stir in the rice. Add the wine and stir until the wine has evaporated. Add 500 ml (17 fl oz/2 cups) hot stock, then cook, stirring frequently, for about 5–7 minutes until liquid is absorbed. Add another 500 ml (17 fl oz/2 cups) hot stock and repeat process. Add remaining hot stock and stir in the asparagus pieces. Stir until liquid is mostly absorbed and rice is creamy and tender. Stir in the butter, parmesan and 2 teaspoons of the lemon rind.

Meanwhile, pat fish fillets dry with paper towels. Put the polenta on a flat tray and coat fish fillets with polenta, shaking off any excess. Heat the remaining oil in a large frying pan over medium heat. When hot add the fillets and cook for 3–4 minutes, turning once, or until crisp and cooked through. Drain on paper towels.

To serve, combine the mascarpone, thyme leaves and remaining lemon rind in a small bowl. Divide the risotto among four serving plates, top each with a fish fillet and add a spoonful of thyme mascarpone. Serve immediately.

Add 155 g (5½ oz/1 cup) frozen peas to the risotto instead of the asparagus, if preferred. Cooking time for the fish will vary, depending upon thickness so if you use a different fish to basa, it may take longer to cook through.

Lamb shanks with almonds, sherry and brown rice

2 tablespoons olive oil
8 x 250 g (9 oz) lamb shanks, French-
    trimmed (ask your butcher to do this)
    or 4 large lamb shanks
2 red onions, thinly sliced
2 red capsicums (peppers), thinly sliced
2 garlic cloves, crushed
125 ml (4 fl oz/½ cup) dry sherry
500 ml (17 fl oz/2 cups) chicken stock
30 g (1 oz/¼ cup) raisins
30 g (1 oz/¼ cup) slivered almonds
220 g (7¾ oz/1 cup) brown rice
1 small handful flat-leaf (Italian) parsley,
    finely chopped

Preheat the oven to 180°C (350°F/Gas 4).

Heat the oil in a large ovenproof saucepan over medium heat. Add the lamb shanks and cook, turning often, for 2–3 minutes or until browned all over. Remove from the pan and set aside. Add the onion and capsicum to the pan. Cook for 4–5 minutes or until softened, then add the garlic, stirring with a wooden spoon for another 3 minutes. Add the sherry to the pan, stirring to remove any sediment from the base of the pan. Increase the heat to high and bring to the boil for 2 minutes. Add the chicken stock and return to the boil for 3 minutes. Remove from heat, add the lamb shanks and raisins, cover, then transfer to the oven and cook for 1¼ hours or until the meat is tender and falling off the bone.

Place the almonds on a baking tray and roast in the oven for 5 minutes or until golden. Set aside to cool.

Meanwhile, place the brown rice in a sieve under cold running water until the water runs clear. Place in a saucepan with 750 ml (26 fl oz/3 cups) cold water. Cover the saucepan, place over a low heat and cook for 40 minutes or until the water has evaporated and the rice is tender. Remove from heat and stir in parsley.

Divide the rice between the serving plates, top with lamb shanks, spoon over pan juices and serve sprinkled with almonds.

Preparation time: 30 minutes   **Cooking time:** 1 hour 40 minutes   **Serves:** 4

Preparation time: 40 minutes ❋ **Cooking time:** 30 minutes ❋ **Serves:** 4

Veal scaloppine with potato-fennel salad and tuna mayonnaise

2 tablespoons torn sage leaves
60 ml (2 fl oz/¼ cup) olive oil
4 x 175 g (6 oz) veal scaloppine fillets
  or schnitzels, trimmed
20 g (¾ oz) unsalted butter
1 tablespoon capers, rinsed and drained

Potato-fennel salad

1 fennel bulb (about 430 g/15¼ oz)
60 ml (2 fl oz/¼ cup) extra virgin olive oil
1 tablespoon red wine vinegar
1 teaspoon dijon mustard
1 garlic clove, crushed with a little sea salt
250 g (9 oz) new potatoes, cooked and
  drained and quartered
45 g (1¾ oz/¼ cup) small green olives

Tuna mayonnaise

180 g (6 oz/¾ cup)
  whole-egg mayonnaise
185 g (6½ oz) tin tuna in oil, drained
  and flaked
4 anchovy fillets, finely chopped

To make the tuna mayonnaise, combine all the ingredients in a food processor and process until smooth. Season to taste with sea salt and freshly ground black pepper and thin with a little water if desired. Cover and stand at room temperature until ready to serve.

To make the potato-fennel salad, trim fennel, reserving 1 tablespoon chopped fronds. Cook the fennel bulb in boiling salted water for 15 minutes or until just tender. Drain well and pat dry with paper towels. Cut the fennel in half, then into thin wedges. Heat the oil in a large non-stick frying pan over medium heat. Cook the fennel for 5 minutes, turning once, until light golden. Remove the fennel from the pan, draining well and reserving the oil in the pan. Whisk the reserved oil, vinegar, mustard and garlic in a bowl. Add the potatoes, olives, fennel and reserved fennel fronds, add freshly ground black pepper to taste and toss until well combined.

Meanwhile, for the scaloppine, combine the sage leaves and oil in a large bowl, add the veal and turn to coat. Cover and stand at cool room temperature for 15 minutes, then drain meat well. Melt the butter in a frying pan just large enough to hold the veal in a single layer without overlapping. When it begins to sizzle add the veal. Cook for 1–2 minutes each side or until golden and just cooked through; take care not to overcook the veal or it will be tough. Transfer the meat to warmed plates, dollop tuna mayonnaise on top and scatter with capers. Serve immediately with the warm salad on the side.

Tuna mayonnaise can be made a day ahead and kept covered in the refrigerator. Bring to room temperature to serve.

Spinach fish rolls with lemon-butter sauce

If you like, you can substitute the sauce with a bought hollandaise sauce. Any long flat fresh or frozen fish fillets that can be rolled easily can be used for this recipe.

250 g (9 oz) English spinach (about 1 bunch), washed, dried and stalks removed
15 g (½ oz) butter
1 small red onion, finely chopped
1 garlic clove, chopped
½ teaspoon freshly grated nutmeg
750 g (1 lb 10 oz) potatoes, peeled and cut into 5 mm (¼ inch) slices
80 ml (2½ fl oz/⅓ cup) olive oil
6 x 175 g (6 oz) thin fish fillets, such as basa, skin removed
1 tablespoon finely chopped flat-leaf (Italian) parsley

Lemon-butter sauce
125 g (4½ oz) butter
4 egg yolks
1 tablespoon lemon juice

To make the lemon-butter sauce, slowly melt the butter in a small saucepan over low heat, then cook for 1–2 minutes or until very hot. Place the egg yolks and lemon juice in a food processor or blender and process until well combined. With the motor running add the hot butter in a thin, steady stream and process until mixture is thick and emulsified. Season to taste with sea salt and freshly ground black pepper. Transfer to a bowl, cover with foil and stand at warm room temperature.

To make the filling, finely chop the spinach leaves. Heat the butter in a frying pan over medium heat and add the onion and garlic. Cook for 2–3 minutes or until slightly softened, then add the spinach and nutmeg and stir for 2–3 minutes or until spinach is wilted. Cool.

Meanwhile, preheat the oven to 180°C (350°F/Gas 4). Place the potatoes in a large roasting pan in a single layer or slightly overlapping and drizzle with the olive oil. Pat the fish fillets dry with paper towels. Divide the spinach filling among the fish, spreading it evenly over the skinned side of each fillet. Roll up each fillet from the tail end. Place rolled fillets on the potatoes in the roasting pan, placing them against each other so they don't unroll. Cover the pan with foil and bake for 20 minutes or until cooked. To serve, arrange the potatoes and fish rolls in the centre of each serving plate, spoon over lemon-butter sauce and top with chopped parsley. Serve any remaining sauce separately.

Preparation time: 20 minutes **Cooking time:** 30 minutes **Serves:** 6

Preparation time: 35 minutes ✳ **Cooking time:** 1 hour 20 minutes ✳ **Serves:** 4

Root vegetable and goat's cheese tian with hazelnut butter

450 g (1 lb/about 2) beetroot
 (beets), trimmed
1 litre (35 fl oz/4 cups) vegetable
 or chicken stock
450 g (1 lb/about 2) turnips, peeled and
 sliced into 2 mm ($^1/_{16}$ inch) slices
250 g (9 oz/about 1) sweet potato, peeled
 and sliced into 2 mm ($^1/_{16}$ inch) slices
350 g (12 oz/about 1) parsnip, peeled
 and sliced into 2 mm ($^1/_{16}$ inch) slices
2 teaspoons extra virgin olive oil
1 large leek, white part only, thinly sliced
2 garlic cloves, crushed
2 teaspoons finely chopped thyme
75 g (2¾ oz) pancetta (about 4 slices),
 cut into quarters
150 g (5½ oz/1¼ cups) crumbled
 goat's cheese

Hazelnut butter
35 g (1¼ oz/¼ cup) shelled roasted
 hazelnuts, finely chopped
50 g (1¾ oz) butter
½ teaspoon finely grated lemon rind

Preheat the oven to 200°C (400°F/Gas 6). Wrap the beetroot in foil and place on a baking tray. Bake for 35–40 minutes or until tender when pierced with a knife. Set aside to cool. Peel and slice into 2 mm ($^1/_{16}$ inch) thick slices.

Meanwhile bring the stock to the boil in a saucepan over high heat. Add the sliced turnip, sweet potato and parsnip. Cover, reduce heat to medium and simmer for 7–10 minutes or until the vegetables are just tender. Drain well.

Reduce the oven to 180°C (350°C/Gas 4). Heat the oil in a frying pan over medium–low heat. Add the leek and cook, stirring, for 2–3 minutes or until tender. Add the garlic and thyme, and cook for 1 minute. Divide the leek mixture among four 14 x 10 cm (5½ x 4 inch) ovenproof dishes, spreading to evenly cover the bases. Cover the leek mixture with rows of overlapping slices of beetroot, turnip, sweet potato, parsnip and pancetta. Sprinkle with goat's cheese and season with sea salt and freshly ground black pepper. Bake for 25 minutes.

To make the hazelnut butter, heat a small saucepan over medium heat. Add all the ingredients and cook, whisking, until foaming. Remove from heat.

Turn the tians out onto serving plates, spoon over the hazelnut butter and serve immediately.

Try this dish with a mild blue cheese instead of the goat's cheese and chopped blanched almonds instead of the hazelnuts.

Roast spatchcock with braised peas and lettuce

If you prefer, you can use four large chicken marylands (leg quarters) instead of the spatchcocks – the cooking time and temperature will be the same. Pressing the herbed butter between the skin and breast meat helps add flavour and baste the meat, so there is no need to turn spatchcocks while roasting.

4 x 450 g (1 lb) spatchcocks (poussins)
1 small handful thyme sprigs
50 g (1¾ oz) unsalted butter, softened
1 lemon, quartered
2 tablespoons olive oil
85 g (3 oz) paper-thin slices pancetta (about 8)
boiled new potatoes, to serve

Braised peas and lettuce
1 tablespoon olive oil
1 onion, finely chopped
1 garlic clove, crushed
310 g (11 oz/2 cups) frozen peas
200 ml (7 fl oz) chicken stock
¼ teaspoon freshly grated nutmeg
½ iceberg or cos (romaine) lettuce (about 350g/12 oz), outer leaves trimmed, finely shredded

Preheat the oven to 200°C (400°F/Gas 6). Cut necks off spatchcocks, then pat spatchcocks dry inside and out with paper towels. Remove a teaspoon of leaves from thyme sprigs. Mix leaves with butter. Using your fingers, lift the skin away from the breast meat on each side, to form 2 pockets. Smear a quarter of the butter mixture under the skin of each spatchcock, then pat skin back into place. Rub each bird with a lemon quarter and season with sea salt and freshly ground black pepper. Push lemon pieces and remaining thyme into cavities.

Heat oil in an ovenproof frying pan large enough to fit spatchcocks. Fry pancetta each side for about 1 minute or until golden, then remove and drain on paper towel. Place spatchcocks in pan and cook, turning often, for 7–10 minutes or until golden all over. Season to taste. Transfer pan to oven and roast for 12–15 minutes or until cooked through. Remove from pan to a warmed platter, breast side down, cover with foil and rest for 10 minutes in a warm place.

Meanwhile, to make braised peas and lettuce, heat oil in a heavy-based saucepan over a medium heat. Add onion and cook, stirring, for 10 minutes or until lightly caramelised. Stir in garlic and peas. Add stock and 250 ml (9 fl oz/1 cup) water and bring to the boil. Cook for 15 minutes. Using a hand-held blender or food processor, coarsely purée peas. Return peas to pan over a low heat. Add nutmeg and lettuce and stir for 1 minute or until lettuce has wilted.

Crumble pancetta over spatchcock and serve with boiled new potatoes and braised peas and lettuce on the side.

⁕ Preparation time: 30 minutes   **⁕ Cooking time:** 30 minutes   **⁕ Serves:** 4

Preparation time: 30 minutes
plus 30 minutes marinating time

Cooking time: 3 hours 40 minutes

Serves: 6

Roast pork neck with braised cabbage and apple remoulade

2 tablespoons olive oil
1 tablespoon ground fennel seeds
2 garlic cloves, crushed
finely grated rind and juice of 1 lemon
1.4 kg (3 lb 2 oz) piece pork neck
500 ml (17 fl oz/2 cups) chicken stock

Braised cabbage

30 g (1 oz) soft butter
1 tablespoon olive oil
1 onion, finely chopped
1.4 kg (3 lb 2 oz) red cabbage (about 1),
   trimmed and thinly sliced
2 teaspoons wholegrain mustard
95 g (3¼ oz/½ cup lightly packed)
   brown sugar
500 ml (17 fl oz/2 cups) chicken stock
50 ml (1¾ fl oz) red wine vinegar

Apple remoulade

1 small fennel bulb, very thinly sliced
   (or shaved on a mandolin)
350 g (12 oz) granny smith apples
   (about 2), peeled and cut into
   thin matchsticks
2 tablespoons lemon juice
125 g (4 oz/½ cup)
   whole-egg mayonnaise
2 teaspoons wholegrain mustard
2 tablespoons chopped flat-leaf
   (Italian) parsley

Preheat the oven to 150°C (300°F/Gas 2). In a small bowl combine 1 tablespoon of the olive oil, fennel seeds, garlic and lemon rind and juice, and mix well. Rub the mixture evenly over the pork neck and season well with sea salt and freshly ground black pepper. Set aside for 30 minutes for flavours to develop.

Heat the remaining oil in a large, heavy-based frying pan over medium heat. Add the pork and cook for 5–7 minutes, turning often, until golden all over. Add the chicken stock, bring to a simmer, then transfer meat and stock to a roasting pan. Cover dish with foil and bake for 2½ hours. Remove foil, baste pork with juices then bake, uncovered, for 1 hour or until cooked through and tender. Remove pork from dish to a large plate and loosely cover with foil. Rest in a warm place for 10 minutes.

Meanwhile, to make the braised cabbage, heat the butter and oil in a large saucepan over medium heat. Add the onion and cook, stirring, for 3–5 minutes or until softened. Add the cabbage, mustard, sugar and chicken stock and bring to the boil. Cover, reduce heat and simmer for 10 minutes, then add the vinegar and cook, covered, for another 30 minutes or until the cabbage is tender.

For the remoulade, place fennel, apple and lemon juice in a small bowl and mix well. In a separate bowl combine the mayonnaise, mustard and parsley with 1 tablespoon of boiling water. Stir mayonnaise through fennel and apple. Season to taste.

Serve sliced pork neck with braised cabbage and apple remoulade.

Lamb with bean compote and tomato-basil cream

If you like your lamb a little pink, cook it for 1 hour and 15 minutes. If you like it well done, cook as described above but no longer or the meat will be tough and flavourless.

1 x 1.2 kg (2 lb 12 oz) leg of lamb, boned with shank bone left in (ask your butcher to do this)
1.5 litres (52 fl oz/6 cups) chicken stock
1 onion, chopped
2 carrots, chopped
3 rosemary sprigs
6 garlic cloves (2 crushed)
200 g (7 oz) green beans
1 tablespoon olive oil
1 leek, white part only, thinly sliced
1 x 400 g (14 oz) tin cannellini beans, drained and rinsed

Tomato-basil cream
70 g (2½ oz/½ cup) drained semi-dried (sun-blushed) tomatoes, finely chopped
2 garlic cloves, finely chopped
250 g (9 oz/1 cup) sour cream
2 tablespoons finely chopped basil

To make the tomato-basil cream, combine the tomatoes, 2 tablespoons water, garlic and half the sour cream in a food processor and process until smooth. Stir in the remaining sour cream and basil, season to taste with sea salt and freshly ground black pepper and transfer to a small bowl. Cover and refrigerate until ready to serve.

Place the lamb in a large saucepan with the stock and enough cold water to just cover the lamb. Add the onion, carrots, rosemary and 4 whole garlic cloves, bring to the boil, then reduce heat to low, cover pan and cook for 1½ hours. Do not allow mixture to boil or meat will become tough. Remove lamb from pan, cover and keep warm. Reserve 250 ml (9 fl oz/1 cup) of the lamb poaching liquid.

To make the bean compote, cook the green beans in a saucepan of lightly salted water for 5 minutes or until just tender, then drain, plunge into a bowl of cold water, drain well. Heat oil over medium–low heat in a small frying pan. Add leek and the 2 crushed garlic cloves and cook, stirring, for 3–5 minutes or until tender. Add reserved poaching liquid, green beans and cannellini beans and cook for 2 minutes or until heated through. Season to taste.

Cut the lamb into 1 cm (½ inch) slices and serve topped with a dollop of tomato-basil cream and bean compote on the side.

✳ Preparation time: 20 minutes   **✳ Cooking time:** 1 hour 30 minutes   **✳ Serves:** 6

Preparation time: 30 minutes
plus 4 hours marinating time

Cooking time: 4 hours 45 minutes

Serves: 6

Braised oxtail with broad beans and parsnip

2.2 kg (5 lb) oxtail, cut into 4 cm
(1½ inch) pieces and trimmed
of excess fat
750 ml (26 fl oz/3 cups) red wine
4 thyme sprigs
3 garlic cloves, sliced
75 g (2¾ oz/½ cup) plain
(all-purpose) flour
2 teaspoons ground allspice
60 ml (2 fl oz/¼ cup) olive oil
12 baby onions (about 500 g/1 lb 2 oz),
peeled and halved
2 tablespoons tomato paste
(concentrated purée)
750 ml (26 fl oz/3 cups) beef stock
450 g (1 lb/3 cups) frozen broad (fava)
beans, thawed and peeled, or fresh
or frozen peas
1 handful flat-leaf (Italian) parsley,
finely chopped
1.25 kg (2 lb 12 oz) parsnips (about 6),
peeled and cut into 3 mm (⅛ inch)
thick slices
60 g (2¼ oz) butter, melted
1 large handful mixed baby salad leaves

Place the oxtail, wine, thyme and garlic in
a non-metallic bowl. Cover and marinate for
4 hours or overnight.

Preheat the oven to 150°C (300°F/Gas 2).
Drain the marinade from the oxtail and reserve.
Place oxtail, flour, allspice, sea salt and freshly
ground black pepper into a plastic bag and
shake until well coated. Heat 2 tablespoons of
the olive oil in a large, flameproof casserole dish
over a medium–high heat. Add oxtail, in batches,
and cook for 3–4 minutes on each side or until
golden brown. Set meat aside, reserving pan.

Reduce heat to medium–low. Add remaining
olive oil and onions to the pan and cook, stirring,
for 4–5 minutes or until golden. Add the tomato
paste and return oxtail to the pan. Pour in
reserved marinade and stock. Bring to the boil,
then cover and transfer to the oven. Bake for
4 hours or until meat is very tender and falling
from the bone. Remove meat and onions from
the liquid and cool. Remove meat from the bones
and tear into bite-sized pieces. Discard bones.
Increase oven to 180°C (350°F/Gas 4). Strain
the liquid into a small saucepan and cook over a
medium–low heat, skimming to remove any scum
that rises to the surface. Remove from heat and
combine with the meat, broad beans and parsley
in a bowl, season to taste and stir to combine
well. Divide mixture among six 200 ml (7 fl oz)
capacity gratin dishes or ramekins.

Bring a saucepan of salted water to the boil,
add parsnips and cook for 1–2 minutes or until
softened. Drain well and cool slightly, then pat
with paper towels to remove as much moisture
as possible. Place 2 layers of parsnips over meat
mixture in dishes in neat, overlapping rows,
as parsnips will shrink during cooking. Brush
parsnips with melted butter, then place dishes
on a baking tray and bake for 20–25 minutes or
until parsnips are golden. Serve immediately with
salad leaves on the side.

Roast chicken with bread, lemon and rocket salad

1.5 kg (3 lb 5 oz) roasting chicken
6 sage leaves
300 g (10½ oz) day-old ciabatta bread
  (about ½ a loaf)
125 ml (4 fl oz/½ cup) olive oil
3 garlic cloves, thinly sliced
1 small red onion, thinly sliced
2 tablespoons raisins
2 tablespoons caperberries
2 teaspoons finely grated lemon rind
1 small handful flat-leaf (Italian) parsley
90 g (3¼ oz/½ cup) small green
  olives, pitted
1 large handful rocket (arugula)
2 tablespoons white balsamic vinegar

Remove any excess fat from the chicken, then rinse the chicken in cold water and pat dry with paper towels. Slide a finger under the skin of each breast to make a pocket and loosen the skin on the thickest part of the thigh flesh. Place sage in the cavities between the skin and the flesh. Season the chicken with sea salt and freshly ground black pepper, and sprinkle a little extra salt inside the cavity. Cover the chicken with plastic wrap and refrigerate overnight.

Preheat the oven to 240°C (475°F/Gas 8). Remove the chicken from the refrigerator and pat dry with paper towels. Place a 25 x 30 cm (10 x 12 inch) roasting pan in the oven to preheat. When hot, place the chicken in the pan, breast side up, in the middle of the oven and cook for 30 minutes or until the chicken is starting to brown. Turn the chicken over, roast for another 10–15 minutes, then turn breast side up again and cook for another 15 minutes, or until the skin is crisp and the chicken is cooked through.

Meanwhile, slice the bread into four 2 cm (¾ inch) thick slices, then cut into 2 cm (¾ inch) cubes. Place in a roasting pan, drizzle with 2 tablespoons of the olive oil, add the garlic and onion and bake for 10 minutes or until crisp. Remove and set aside.

Remove the chicken from the roasting pan, reserving the cooking juices, and transfer the chicken to a warmed platter. Cover loosely with foil and keep warm. Skim any fat from the cooking juices, then add the juices to the bread and toss to combine.

Place the bread mixture in a large salad bowl with raisins, caperberries, lemon rind, parsley, olives and rocket, and drizzle with the combined balsamic vinegar and remaining oil. Toss to combine, then place on a large serving platter. Cut the chicken into pieces, place on a platter with salad and serve immediately.

Preparation time: 25 minutes
plus overnight marinating

Cooking time: 1 hour

Serves: 4

Preparation time: 45 minutes
plus 20 minutes chilling

Cooking time: 1 hour 10 minutes

Serves: 6

Individual meatloaf Wellingtons with redcurrant-marsala glaze

1 small onion, chopped finely
2 garlic cloves, crushed
600 g (1 lb 5 oz) minced (ground) pork
1 tablespoon tomato paste
  (concentrated purée)
1 tablespoon dijon mustard
1 egg, lightly beaten, plus another
  for brushing pastry
1 teaspoon sea salt
80 g (2¾ oz/1 cup) fresh breadcrumbs
4 sheets frozen butter puff pastry, thawed
green salad or steamed green vegetables,
  to serve

Mushroom duxelle

20 g (¾ oz) butter
3 French shallots, finely chopped
2 garlic cloves, finely chopped
200 g (7 oz) button mushrooms,
  finely chopped

Redcurrant-marsala glaze

150 g (5½ oz/½ cup) redcurrant jelly
60 ml (2 fl oz/¼ cup) dry marsala or
  dry sherry
125 ml (4 fl oz/½ cup) beef stock

Line a large baking tray (40 x 28 cm/16 x 11¼ inches) with baking paper. In a bowl combine the onion, garlic, pork, tomato paste, mustard, egg, salt and ½ teaspoon freshly ground black pepper. Using your hands, knead the mixture until smooth and combined, then add the breadcrumbs and knead again to mix well. Divide the meatloaf mixture into 6 even portions and shape each portion into a small meatloaf, about 7 x 10 cm (2¾ x 4 inches). Place meatloaves on a tray and refrigerate for 20 minutes. Preheat the oven to 220°C (425°F/Gas 7).

For the mushroom duxelle, melt the butter in a small frying pan over low heat. Add the shallots and cook, stirring occasionally, for 4–5 minutes or until soft and golden. Add the garlic and mushrooms and cook for 20 minutes or until the liquid has evaporated and the mixture has thickened. Cool and set aside.

Cut 1 sheet of pastry into 4 cm (1½ inch) wide strips, then cut strips into four 1 cm (½ inch) strips. Place strips on a tray and refrigerate. Working with 1 piece of pastry at a time, cut remaining pastry sheets in half widthways. Place a tablespoon of the mushroom mixture in the centre of each half. Place a meatloaf on top of mushroom mixture. Bring pastry up and over meatloaf (sides will not cover loaf), then roll up to enclose meat, forming a neat parcel, pressing any joins to seal. Place on a tray and repeat with remaining pastry, mushrooms and meatloaves. Brush all over with lightly beaten egg. Decorate tops of meatloaves with reserved pastry strips, as desired. Brush tops with egg and bake for 30–40 minutes or until pastry is crisp and meatloaves are cooked through.

For the redcurrant-marsala glaze, place all the ingredients in a small saucepan and cook over medium–low heat for 6–7 minutes or until reduced and thickened slightly. Serve meatloaves topped with a little of the glaze and green salad or steamed vegetables on the side.

You can make these with chicken or turkey mince as well, exchange the mushroom mixture with a slice of camembert cheese.

Grilled swordfish with onion jam and wine potatoes

If swordfish is not available, try mackerel, kingfish or another firm, full-flavoured fish. You'll need to adjust the cooking time accordingly. For pinker, more 'winey' potatoes, replace the water with another cup of shiraz.

500 g (1 lb 2 oz) new, or other small, boiling potatoes (about 10)
500 ml (17 fl oz/2 cups) shiraz or other fruity red wine
20 g (¾ oz) butter
4 x 200 g (7 oz) swordfish fillets
60 ml (2 fl oz/¼ cup) olive oil
1 fennel bulb, trimmed and very thinly sliced
1 small red onion, finely sliced
1 tablespoon capers, drained
1 small handful flat-leaf (Italian) parsley, chopped
2 teaspoons lemon juice, or to taste

Onion jam

1 large red onion, thinly sliced
50 ml (1¾ fl oz) lemon juice
½ teaspoon fennel seeds
1 teaspoon brown mustard seeds (optional)
2 tablespoons extra virgin olive oil
2 tablespoons caster (superfine) sugar
1 teaspoon finely grated lemon rind

To make the onion jam, combine the onion and lemon juice in a small stainless-steel saucepan and stand for 5 minutes. Heat a small, heavy-based frying pan to medium–low, add the fennel seeds and mustard seeds, if using, and toast, shaking the pan occasionally, for 1–2 minutes or until just fragrant. Add the seeds, oil and sugar to the onion in the pan, bring to the boil over medium heat, then reduce heat to low and cook for 15 minutes or until onion has softened and mixture has thickened. Cool, then stir in lemon rind.

Meanwhile, combine the potatoes in a saucepan with the wine and 250 ml (9 fl oz/1 cup) water, then bring to the boil. Cook over medium heat for 15 minutes or until potatoes are tender, then drain. Return the potatoes to the saucepan and crush slightly using the back of a wooden spoon. Add the butter, cover and keep warm.

Heat a chargrill pan or a large, heavy-based frying pan over medium heat. Brush fish on both sides with half of the oil and season to taste with sea salt and freshly ground black pepper. Place fish, skin side down, on plate or in pan and cook for 2–3 minutes. Turn and cook for another 2–3 minutes or until just cooked through and remove from the heat. Fish should still be a little pink in the middle.

In a small bowl combine the fennel, onion, capers and parsley and toss with the lemon juice and remaining oil. Season to taste. To serve, divide the fish and potatoes among warmed plates, top fish with a teaspoon of onion jam and serve with the fennel salad.

Preparation time: 30 minutes   **Cooking time:** 40 minutes   **Serves:** 4

✳ Preparation time: 20 minutes   **✳ Cooking time:** 1 hour 10 minutes   **✳ Serves:** 6

Chicken drumsticks with pumpkin curry and tamarind chutney

1 red onion, chopped
2 garlic cloves, chopped
1 green chilli, halved and seeded
1 tablespoon grated ginger
½ teaspoon ground turmeric
1 teaspoon ground coriander
1 teaspoon ground cumin
1 large handful coriander (cilantro) (about
   1 bunch), stems only
2 tablespoons vegetable oil
1 teaspoon brown mustard seeds
250 ml (9 fl oz/1 cup) coconut milk
800 g (1 lb 12 oz) pumpkin (winter
   squash), peeled, seeded and cut into
   4 cm (1½ inch) pieces
250 g (9 oz) cherry tomatoes (1 punnet)
12 chicken drumsticks
90 g (3¼ oz/2 cups) baby spinach

Tamarind chutney
125 ml (4 fl oz/½ cup) tamarind purée
80 g (2¾ oz/½ cup) pitted, chopped dates
1 teaspoon ground cumin
¾ teaspoon ground ginger
2 tablespoons brown sugar

To make the tamarind chutney, combine all the ingredients and 250 ml (9 fl oz/1 cup) water in a small saucepan over medium heat and bring to the boil. Reduce heat to low and cook for 20 minutes, or until the mixture is thick and has a jam-like consistency. Remove from the heat and set aside to cool.

Preheat the oven to 200°C (400°F/Gas 6). Combine the onion, garlic, chilli, ginger, turmeric, ground coriander, cumin and coriander stems in a food processor. Process until a smooth paste forms, adding 1 tablespoon of the oil. If necessary, add 1 tablespoon of water for a smoother consistency.

Heat the remaining oil in a large frying pan over medium heat. Add the mustard seeds and cook, stirring, until they start to pop, then add the spice paste and cook, stirring constantly, for 2 minutes or until fragrant. Add the coconut milk and stir to combine well. Place the pumpkin in a roasting pan and pour half of the curry mixture over, tossing to coat well. Season with sea salt and freshly ground black pepper. Roast for 40 minutes, add tomatoes and roast for 5 minutes or until tomatoes just start to collapse. Transfer to a bowl and toss gently with the spinach leaves.

Meanwhile, using a large, sharp knife cut the knuckle end from each drumstick. Place chicken in a roasting pan, add the remaining curry mixture and toss to coat well. Season to taste, then roast for 30–35 minutes or until cooked through. Divide the pumpkin curry among the serving plates, place 2 drumsticks on each plate and serve with the chutney passed separately.

If you're running short on time, the chicken and curry taste just as good served with wedges of lime instead of the tamarind chutney. For a little extra colour and flavour, garnish with coriander leaves.

Coconut beef with pineapple and sweet potato salad

125 ml (4 fl oz/½ cup) coconut cream
¾ teaspoon ground turmeric
1 garlic clove, crushed
2 teaspoons grated ginger
1 teaspoon light soy sauce
4 x 130 g (4¾ oz) beef minute steaks

Pineapple and sweet potato salad
200 g (7 oz) pineapple (about ¼ small
  pineapple), peeled, cored and sliced
Vegetable oil, for brushing
350 g (12 oz) sweet potato (about 1),
  thinly sliced
2 tablespoons roasted peanuts,
  roughly chopped
1 red bird's eye chilli, seeded and chopped
1 large handful coriander (cilantro) leaves
150 g (5½ oz/1⅔ cups) bean sprouts
2 tablespoons lime juice
1½ tablespoons brown sugar
1 tablespoon fish sauce

In a large bowl combine coconut cream, turmeric, garlic, ginger, and soy sauce. Add beef and toss to coat, cover, then refrigerate for at least 3 hours.

About 15 minutes before you are ready to cook the beef, make the pineapple and sweet potato salad. Heat a chargrill pan over medium heat until it reaches smoking point. Brush pineapple slices lightly with oil and chargrill each side for 2–3 minutes or until golden. Set aside in a large bowl. Repeat process with the sweet potato, cooking it for 3–4 minutes each side, or until tender and lightly charred. Toss together with the peanuts, chilli, coriander leaves and bean sprouts. Place lime juice, brown sugar and fish sauce in a small bowl and stir until sugar dissolves, then toss through the salad.

To cook the steaks, chargrill 1–2 minutes each side until browned and just cooked through; take care not to overcook the meat or it will be tough. Slice meat into 2 cm (¾ inch) slices on the diagonal.

To serve, divide the salad among plates, top with a few slices of meat and serve immediately.

Preparation time: 30 minutes
plus at least 3 hours marinating time

Cooking time: 25 minutes

Serves: 4

Preparation time: 15 minutes   **Cooking time:** 20 minutes   **Serves:** 4

Miso and sesame pork with noodle, daikon and seaweed salad

1 tablespoon vegetable oil

2 x 300 g (10½ oz) pork fillets

1 garlic clove, crushed

2 tablespoons white miso paste

1 tablespoon sesame seeds

150 g (5½ oz) dried soba noodles
(available from Asian section
of the supermarket)

½ teaspoon dashi powder (available from
Asian section of the supermarket)

2 tablespoons mirin

1½ tablespoons soy sauce

¼ teaspoon rice vinegar

1½ teaspoons finely grated ginger

½ teaspoon sesame oil

50 g (1¾ oz) snow pea (mangetout)
sprouts, trimmed

100 g (3½ oz) daikon, peeled and cut
into thin matchsticks

1 sheet toasted seaweed (nori), cut into
5 mm (¼ inch) thick shreds

Preheat the oven to 180°C (350°F/Gas 4). Heat the oil in a frying pan over medium–high heat and cook the pork for 3–4 minutes, turning, until browned all over. Remove from heat and cool slightly. Combine the garlic with the miso paste and brush mixture evenly over the pork. Sprinkle sesame seeds over the pork, pressing in gently so they stick to the miso paste. Place onto a baking paper-lined baking tray. Roast pork for 12–15 minutes or until just cooked through. Remove to a plate, cover with foil and keep warm.

Meanwhile, bring a saucepan of water to the boil then cook the soba noodles for 4 minutes or according to packet instructions; drain well. Combine dashi powder and 1½ tablespoons warm water in a small bowl and stir to dissolve dashi. In a large bowl combine dashi mixture, mirin, soy sauce, rice vinegar, ginger and sesame oil, then add noodles, snow pea sprouts and daikon and toss to combine well.

To serve, twirl portions of the noodle mixture onto serving plates and top with the sliced pork. Sprinkle with the shredded nori and serve immediately.

Desserts

Mango-meringue roulade • Apple tarts with rosemary syrup • Bread and butter pudding with red wine sauce • Strawberry vanilla ice cream terrine • Roasted fruits with maple-ricotta cream • Buttermilk panna cotta with caramelised oranges • Carrot-apricot puddings with orange custard • Lemon delicious with raspberry cream • White chocolate and passionfruit cheesecake • Poached pears in coffee syrup with vanilla cream • Chocolate sticky date puddings with caramel sauce • Cornmeal crepes with plums and honey cream • Cherry and almond parfait • Pineapple in star-anise syrup with coconut ice cream • Chocolate-caramel tarts • Spiced wine jelly • Hazelnut vacherin with chocolate-coffee cream • Lime and coconut shortcakes • Berry sago pudding • Rice flour pudding with rhubarb-rosewater compote • Apple terrine • Peach and nutmeg crème brûlée • Pear, almond and elderflower crumble • Gingerbread soufflé • Vanilla rice tart with apricot purée • Banana semifreddo with rum-caramel sauce

Mango-meringue roulade

5 egg whites, at room temperature
185 g (6½ oz/1 cup lightly packed)
  brown sugar
30 g (1 oz/¼ cup) ground hazelnuts

Filling
250 g (9 oz/1 cup) cream
1 x 425 g (15 oz) tin mango, well drained
1 tablespoon icing (confectioner's) sugar

Preheat the oven to 170°C (325°F/Gas 3). Grease a 24 x 34 cm (9½ x 13½ inch) tin and line with baking paper.

Place the egg whites in a clean bowl and whisk with electric beaters until firm peaks form. Whisking constantly, slowly add the sugar, beating well after each addition, until mixture is firm and glossy. Carefully fold in the hazelnuts using a large metal spoon. Spread mixture evenly into prepared tin. Bake for 8 minutes, then reduce oven temperature to 150°C (300°F/Gas 2) and cook for a further 15 minutes or until firm to the touch. Turn out onto a lightly greased sheet of baking paper. Remove baking paper from the underside of the meringue. Cover the meringue with a clean tea (dish) towel and stand until cool.

To make the filling, place the cream into a large bowl and whisk until firm peaks form. Combine the mango with the icing sugar in a food processor and process until smooth. Add half the mango purée to the cream and fold in gently. Spread the mixture over the cooled meringue and refrigerate remaining mango purée.

Starting from a long side of the meringue and using the paper as a guide, roll the meringue to enclose the filling and form a log. Wrap the roulade carefully in plastic wrap and refrigerate for 1½–2 hours or until ready to serve. Slice into 2 cm (¾ inch) slices and serve with the remaining mango purée drizzled over.

If mangoes are in season, substitute tinned mango with 240 g (8½ oz/ 1¼ cups) chopped fresh mango flesh. If you don't have a 24 x 34 cm (9½ x 13½ inch) tin, place baking paper on a large tray, draw a 24 x 34 cm rectangle on paper and spread meringue over rectangle.

Apple tarts with rosemary syrup

If you like, you can use a pastry brush to spread syrup evenly over tarts.

2 sheets frozen puff pastry, thawed
30 g (1 oz) unsalted butter, softened, plus
   20 g (¾ oz) extra, cut into small cubes
2 tablespoons caster (superfine) sugar
1 teaspoon natural vanilla extract
1 teaspoon finely grated lemon rind
35 g (1¼ oz/⅓ cup) ground almonds
1 teaspoon plain (all-purpose) flour
2 small red apples (about 300 g/10½ oz)
50 ml (1½ fl oz) lemon juice

Rosemary syrup

55 g (2 oz/¼ cup) caster (superfine) sugar
8 small rosemary sprigs, leaves removed
   (about 2 tablespoons)

Preheat the oven to 190°C (375°F/Gas 5). Line a large baking tray with baking paper. Lightly brush 1 pastry sheet with water and place the second sheet on top. Press together gently. Cut the pastry evenly into 4 squares and place on the tray. Knock up pastry edges with the back of a dinner knife to help pastry to rise and flake. Prick all over. Bake for 10 minutes until puffed and just golden. Remove from the oven and gently press down with a tea (dish) towel to remove air puff. Set aside to cool.

Meanwhile, place 30 g (1 oz) butter, 1 tablespoon sugar, vanilla and lemon rind in a small bowl and beat with a wooden spoon until creamy. Stir in the almonds and flour. Peel, quarter and core the apples. Place in a bowl and toss with the lemon juice.

Spread almond mixture over pastry bases, leaving a 1 cm (½ inch) edge all around. Slice the apples thinly and arrange 2 sliced apple quarters on each pastry base, slightly overlapping slices. Sprinkle each pastry with 1 teaspoon of the remaining sugar and dot with extra butter. Bake for 20–25 minutes or until pastry is golden brown.

Meanwhile, to make the rosemary syrup, combine 2 tablespoons water with sugar in a small saucepan over a low heat. Stir to dissolve, then add the rosemary leaves and cook for 2–3 minutes or until mixture becomes syrupy.

Serve the tarts warm or at room temperature, drizzled with syrup.

⁕ Preparation time: 20 minutes **⁕ Cooking time:** 45 minutes **⁕ Serves:** 4

Preparation time: 20 minutes
plus 30 minutes standing time

Cooking time: 1 hour 30 minutes

Serves: 6

Bread and butter pudding with red wine sauce

50 g (1¾ oz) unsalted butter, softened, plus extra, for greasing

300 g (10½ oz) day-old baguette, cut into 1.5 cm (⅝ inch) slices

5 eggs, lightly beaten

80 g (2¾ oz/⅓ cup) caster (superfine) sugar

375 ml (13 fl oz/1½ cups) milk

375 ml (13 fl oz/1½ cups) cream

40 g (1½ oz/⅓ cup) walnuts, roughly chopped

Red wine sauce

500 ml (17 fl oz/2 cups) red wine

1 tablespoon caster (superfine) sugar

40 g (1½ oz/⅓ cup) sultanas (golden raisins)

Preheat the oven to 160°C (315°F/Gas 2–3). Lightly grease a 1.5 litre (52 fl oz/6 cup) capacity, 23 x 14 cm (9 x 5½ inch) ovenproof dish. Lightly butter the baguette slices, then arrange them in neat layers in the dish. Combine the eggs, sugar, milk, cream and walnuts in a bowl and pour over the bread. Allow the pudding to stand for 15 minutes to absorb the liquid, then bake for 50–60 minutes or until firm.

To make the red wine sauce, combine the red wine, sugar and sultanas in a small saucepan over medium heat, bring to the boil and reduce heat to medium–low and cook for 20–25 minutes or until reduced and syrupy.

Cool the pudding for 10–15 minutes, then serve with the red wine sauce drizzled over.

Strawberry vanilla ice cream terrine

2 litres (70 fl oz/8 cups) vanilla bean
   ice cream
750 g (1 lb 10 oz/5 cups) strawberries,
   hulled (3 punnets)
2 tablespoons icing (confectioner's) sugar
1 tablespoon lemon juice
1 teaspoon rosewater, or to taste
1 small handful small mint leaves

Line an 11 cm (4¼ inch) deep, 1.875 litre
(65 fl oz/7½ cup), 10.5 x 21 cm (4 x 8¼ inch)
loaf (bar) tin with plastic wrap, leaving 5 cm
(2 inches) overhanging on the long sides.

Divide the ice cream evenly among 2 stainless-steel bowls. Place one of the bowls back in the freezer, leaving the other to soften slightly.

Combine 500 g (1 lb 2 oz) of the strawberries in a food processor with 1 tablespoon of the icing sugar and the lemon juice and process until a smooth purée forms. Pour the strawberry purée through a fine sieve to remove the seeds, pressing down on the solids to remove as much of the pulp as possible. Using a large metal spoon mix the strained purée and the softened ice cream until thoroughly combined, then freeze for 1 hour.

Remove the vanilla and strawberry ice creams from the freezer. Set aside until starting to soften. Spoon half of the vanilla ice cream into the loaf tin, smoothing the top using the back of the spoon. Top with half of the strawberry ice cream, then repeat with the remaining vanilla and strawberry ice creams. Bring the overhanging plastic wrap over the top of the terrine to cover, then freeze for 4 hours or overnight until firm.

To serve, quarter the remaining strawberries and place in a bowl with the remaining icing sugar and rosewater. Set aside for 30 minutes, then stir in the mint. Turn the terrine out of the loaf tin and remove the plastic wrap. Slice terrine into 3 cm (1¼ inch) thick slices and serve with the strawberry salad.

Preparation time: 40 minutes
plus 5 hours freezing time

Cooking time: nil

Serves: 6

Preparation time: 30 minutes   **Cooking time:** 40 minutes   **Serves:** 4

Roasted fruits with maple-ricotta cream

2 red apples, quartered and cored

2 pears, quartered and cored

4 figs, halved

1½ tablespoons caster (superfine) sugar

8 slices almond bread or similar
  biscuit (cookie)

2 tablespoons shelled pistachio nuts,
  lightly roasted and coarsely chopped

Maple-ricotta cream

250 g (9 oz/1 cup) ricotta cheese

2 tablespoons maple syrup

To make the maple-ricotta cream, beat together the ricotta and maple syrup until smooth and creamy. Chill.

Preheat the oven to 200°C (400°F/Gas 6). Place fruit pieces on a large baking tray lined with baking paper and sprinkle each piece with a little caster sugar. Bake for 30–40 minutes or until fruit is soft and golden. Cooking time will depend on ripeness and size of fruit. Remove any cooked pieces and continue to roast remaining fruit until it is all tender. Cool fruit.

To serve, divide the fruit among four serving plates and serve with biscuits, maple-ricotta cream and a scattering of pistachios. Serve warm or at room temperature.

Try this dish with summer fruit – you'll need 2 large nectarines, halved, stone removed and quartered, 2 large peaches, halved, stone removed and quartered, 4 apricots or plums, halved and stone removed. Scatter the sugar over the top and roast for 20–25 minutes. Instead of pistachios, serve scattered with raspberries. You can roast any combination of fruits. You'll need 5–6 pieces of fruit per person.

Buttermilk panna cotta with caramelised oranges

While the syrup is cooking, have a cup of cold water and a pastry brush handy. As the syrup splatters on the inside of the saucepan, brush the area down well with cold water to prevent sugar crystals forming. You can make the syrup up to 1 week in advance and store it in an airtight container in the fridge. Use left-over syrup to spoon over strawberries, raspberries or stone fruit – it's heavenly.

375 ml (13 fl oz/1½ cups) buttermilk
1 tablespoon powdered gelatine
300 ml (10½ fl oz) cream
125 g (4½ oz) caster (superfine) sugar
½ teaspoon natural vanilla extract

Caramelised oranges

230 g (8 oz/1 cup) caster
  (superfine) sugar
3 oranges or 5 blood oranges,
  peeled and all white pith
  removed, thinly sliced

To make the caramelised oranges, place the sugar and 125 ml (4 fl oz/½ cup) boiling water in a saucepan and stir over low heat until the sugar is dissolved. Bring to the boil and cook until syrup is a deep caramel colour. Remove from heat. Working quickly and taking care as mixture will spit, add 125 ml (4 fl oz/½ cup) water to caramel. Swirl the pan to combine well, then place the caramel over low heat and stir until smooth. Place the orange slices in a large, heatproof bowl and pour syrup over. Set aside until cool.

Place 125 ml (4 fl oz/½ cup) of the buttermilk in a small bowl and sprinkle the gelatine over. Leave until the gelatine softens.

Place the cream and sugar in a saucepan and while stirring, bring almost to the boil. Add the remaining buttermilk and vanilla and heat again but do not allow to boil. Remove from heat, stand for 5 minutes to cool slightly, then add the gelatine mixture and stir until the gelatine has dissolved. Leave to cool for 10 minutes, then divide the mixture among six 125 ml (4 fl oz/½ cup) capacity moulds that have been rinsed with cold water. Refrigerate overnight. To serve, dip each mould briefly into a bowl of hot water to loosen the panna cotta, then turn out onto plates and serve with caramelised oranges.

Preparation time: 30 minutes
plus overnight chilling

Cooking time: 15 minutes

Serves: 6

Preparation time: 20 minutes   **Cooking time:** 35 minutes   **Serves:** 6

Carrot-apricot puddings with orange custard

60 g (2¼ oz/⅓ cup) finely chopped
   dried apricots
2 tablespoons apricot jam
2 eggs
125 ml (4 fl oz/½ cup) sunflower oil,
   plus extra, for greasing
95 g (3¼ oz/½ cup, lightly packed)
   brown sugar
1 tablespoon golden syrup (dark
   corn syrup)
90 g (3¼ oz) carrot (about 1), peeled
   and finely grated
150 g (5½ oz/1 cup) plain
   (all-purpose) flour
3 teaspoons baking powder

Orange custard

375 ml (13 fl oz/1½ cups) purchased
   prepared custard
3 teaspoons finely grated orange rind
2 teaspoons orange juice or 1 teaspoon
   orange flower water

To make the orange custard, combine custard, orange rind and juice or flower water in a bowl and stir to combine well. Set aside.

Preheat the oven to 180°C (350°F/Gas 4). Grease six 200 ml (7 fl oz) capacity ramekins or ovenproof moulds and line bases with a circle of baking paper.

Put the apricots in a small bowl and pour over 2 tablespoons boiling water. Stand for 10 minutes or until softened, then stir in the apricot jam. Divide the mixture among the ramekins.

Combine the eggs, oil, sugar and syrup in a medium bowl and, using electric beaters, whisk mixture until thick and pale. Gently stir in the carrot. Sift the flour and baking powder into a small bowl, then gently fold into the egg mixture until combined.

Divide mixture among ramekins, then cover each tightly with a piece of lightly oiled foil. Put in a baking dish and pour in boiling water to come halfway up sides of ramekins. Bake for 35 minutes or until puddings are golden and firm to touch. Remove from baking dish, take off foil and cool slightly. Turn out onto serving plates and serve warm with orange custard.

Lemon delicious with raspberry cream

50 g (1¾ oz) butter, melted, plus extra, for greasing
185 g (6½ oz) caster (superfine) sugar
1 teaspoon finely grated lemon rind
30 g (1 oz/¼ cup) self-raising flour, sifted
60 ml (2 fl oz/¼ cup) lemon juice
3 eggs, separated
310 ml (10¾ fl oz/1¼ cups) milk
250 ml (9 fl oz/1 cup) cream
1 tablespoon icing (confectioner's) sugar, sifted
75 g (2½ oz/½ cup) frozen raspberries, thawed and crushed

Preheat the oven to 180°C (350°F/Gas 4). Lightly grease six 250 ml (9 fl oz/1 cup) capacity ramekins or ovenproof cups. Combine 90 g (3¼ oz) of the caster sugar, lemon rind and flour in a bowl and mix well. In another bowl combine the lemon juice, melted butter, egg yolks and milk and whisk until smooth. Add the milk mixture to the flour mixture and mix until a batter is formed.

Place the egg whites in a clean dry mixing bowl and, using electric beaters, whisk until soft peaks forms. Whisking continuously, slowly add the remaining sugar and whisk until firm peaks form. Add the meringue to the lemon mixture and fold gently until combined.

Divide the mixture among ramekins or cups and place in a deep baking tray. Pour boiling water into tray until it reaches a third of the way up the sides of the ramekins. Place in the oven carefully and bake for 25–30 minutes.

Meanwhile, whisk the cream in a small bowl until thick, stir in the icing sugar and fold through the crushed raspberries.

Serve puddings topped with raspberry cream.

Preparation time: 20 minutes　　**Cooking time:** 25 minutes　　**Serves:** 6

Preparation time: 30 minutes
plus 1 hour 30 minutes standing time

Cooking time: 1 hour

Serves: 10–12

White chocolate and passionfruit cheesecake

150 g (5½ oz) plain sweet digestive
  biscuits (cookies), broken
90 g (3¼ oz/1 cup) desiccated coconut
80 g (2¾ oz) unsalted butter, melted
250 g (9 oz) good quality white
  chocolate, chopped
500 g (1 lb 2 oz) cream cheese, softened
250 g (9 oz/1 cup) sour cream
170 g (5¾ oz/¾ cup) caster
  (superfine) sugar
2 teaspoons natural vanilla extract
3 eggs, lightly beaten
2 x 170 ml (5½ fl oz) tins passionfruit
  pulp

Preheat the oven to 160°C (315°F/Gas 2–3).
Line the base of a 22 cm (8½ inches) diameter
springform tin with baking paper.

Place the biscuits in a food processor and
process until they resemble breadcrumbs. Add
the coconut and melted butter and process until
well combined. Press the mixture evenly over the
base of the pan, then refrigerate for 30 minutes.

Place the white chocolate in a small heatproof
bowl, then place the bowl over a small saucepan
of simmering water, taking care that the water
does not touch the base of the bowl. Heat until
the chocolate has melted, then remove from heat
and stir until smooth. Set aside until cool.

Place the cream cheese, sour cream, sugar
and vanilla in a food processor bowl. Process
until smooth, add the eggs and process until
just combined. Take care not to over-process the
eggs. Add half the passionfruit and chocolate
and, using the pulse button, process until just
combined. Pour the mixture over the biscuit base
in the tin, smoothing the top even.

Place a dish of boiling water in the bottom
of the oven to help prevent cheesecake cracking,
then bake the cheesecake for 1 hour or until
just firm in the centre. Turn the oven off, open
the door slightly and cool the cake in the oven
for 1 hour. Remove, cool to room temperature,
then chill. Serve drizzled with the extra
passionfruit pulp.

Poached pears in coffee syrup with vanilla cream

60 ml (2 fl oz/¼ cup) double-strength espresso coffee

285 g (10 oz/1¼ cups) caster (superfine) sugar, plus 2 teaspoons extra

1 vanilla bean, split and seeds scraped (optional)

4 firm, ripe beurre bosc pears, peeled, stems attached

1 tablespoon Tia Maria, or other coffee-flavoured liqueur (optional)

250 g (9 oz/1 cup) thick (double/heavy) cream

1 teaspoon natural vanilla extract

Combine the coffee, sugar, vanilla seeds and scraped bean, if using, and 700 ml (24 fl oz) water in a saucepan small enough to fit pears snugly. Bring to the boil over medium–low heat, then reduce heat to low and cook, stirring often, for 5 minutes or until sugar has dissolved. Meanwhile, using an apple corer or a teaspoon, remove core from the base end of each pear, creating a tunnel through the pear but taking care not to push all the way through to the stem end. Add pears to the liquid in the saucepan, adding a little water if they are not quite covered. Bring to the boil over medium–low heat, then cover pan, reduce heat to low and cook, turning the pears often, for 15–20 minutes or until pears are tender. Remove pan from heat and cool pears in syrup. Drain pears, reserving 250 ml (9 fl oz/ 1 cup) syrup.

Place reserved syrup in the saucepan, bring to the boil over medium heat, then cook for 10 minutes or until slightly thickened and syrupy. Add liqueur, if using, then cool.

Whisk the cream in a small bowl until firm peaks form, then stir in the extra sugar and vanilla extract.

To serve, place a pear on each plate and drizzle a little of the coffee syrup over. Spoon cream to the side and serve immediately.

Preparation time: 15 minutes   **Cooking time:** 35 minutes   **Serves:** 4

* **Preparation time:** 20 minutes * **Cooking time:** 25 minutes * **Serves:** 6

Chocolate sticky date puddings with caramel sauce

120 g (4¼ oz/¾ cup) chopped
  pitted dates
1½ teaspoons bicarbonate of soda
  (baking soda)
50 g (1¾ oz) unsalted butter, softened
60 g (2¼ oz/⅓ cup lightly packed)
  brown sugar
1 teaspoon natural vanilla extract
1 large egg
110 g (3¾ oz/¾ cup) self-raising flour
100 g (3½ oz/⅔ cup) chopped
  dark chocolate
thick (double/heavy) cream, to serve

Caramel sauce
140 g (5 oz/¾ cup lightly packed)
  brown sugar
200 ml (7 fl oz) cream
75 g (2½ oz) unsalted butter

To make the caramel sauce, place the sugar, cream and butter into a small saucepan over a low heat. Stir until combined and sugar has dissolved. Do not boil.

Preheat the oven to 180°C (350°F/ Gas 4). Lightly grease six 125 ml (4 fl oz/½ cup) ramekins. Place the dates and 185 ml (6 fl oz/¾ cup) water in a small saucepan over medium–high heat. Bring to the boil, reduce heat to medium–low and cook for 3 minutes. Remove from heat, stir in bicarbonate of soda and allow to cool.

Beat the butter and sugar until pale and creamy. Add vanilla and egg, beating well. Gently stir in the flour, chocolate and date mixture. Divide mixture evenly among ramekins. Bake for 15 minutes or until puddings are risen and just firm to the touch; they will still be slightly sticky in the middle. Immediately run a knife around the side of each dish to loosen puddings. Turn out onto serving plates. Drizzle with the caramel sauce and serve immediately with a dollop of cream.

Cornmeal crepes with plums and honey cream

1 x 825 g (1 lb 13 oz) tin plums
   in syrup
115 g (4 oz/½ cup) caster
   (superfine) sugar
4 green cardamom pods, crushed
100 g (3½ oz/⅔ cup) self-raising
   flour, sifted
85 g (3 oz/⅓ cup) fine polenta
½ teaspoon ground turmeric
250 ml (9 fl oz/1 cup) milk
3 eggs, lightly beaten
1 teaspoon vanilla extract
20 g (¾ oz) butter, melted, plus extra,
   for cooking crepes

Honey cream
250 g (9 oz/1 cup) thick
   (double/heavy) cream
2 tablespoons honey, at room temperature
½ teaspoon finely grated orange rind

Drain the plums well, reserving syrup, and cut plums into halves or quarters. Combine the syrup and sugar in a saucepan and cook over medium heat until sugar has dissolved. Add the cardamom pods and plums and cook for 5 minutes, then remove from heat and set aside to cool.

Meanwhile combine the flour, polenta and turmeric in a bowl. Add the milk, eggs, vanilla and melted butter and whisk until a smooth batter forms. Cover and stand for 15 minutes.

Preheat the oven to 120°C (235°F/Gas ½). Heat a 21 cm (8¼ inch) non-stick frying pan or crepe pan over medium heat, then brush the pan with a little melted butter to lightly coat base. Add 60 ml (2 fl oz/¼ cup) of the batter, swirling to coat the base. Cook over medium heat for 1 minute, or until the surface is dry and the edge is light golden. Using a spatula, turn crepe and cook the other side for 1 minute. Turn out on a plate, cover loosely with foil and keep warm in the oven. Repeat process with the remaining batter, stirring batter frequently as polenta will fall to the base of the bowl. You may need to add a little more milk as mixture will thicken slightly on standing.

To make the honey cream, combine the cream, honey and orange rind in a small bowl and gently stir until well combined.

To serve, fold the crepes loosely into quarters, then place 2 crepes on each serving plate. Spoon the plums and syrup over the crepes, then top each with a spoonful of the honey cream. Serve immediately.

Preparation time: 15 minutes
plus 15 minutes standing time

Cooking time: 20 minutes

Serves: 4

Preparation time: 30 minutes
plus 1 hour 10 minutes chilling time

Cooking time: 10 minutes

Serves: 6

Cherry and almond parfait

600 g (1 lb 5 oz/4 cups) frozen pitted
  cherries, thawed
150 g (5½ oz/⅔ cup) caster
  (superfine) sugar
2 teaspoons cornflour (cornstarch)
250 g (9 oz/1 cup) cream
  cheese, chopped
Finely grated rind of 1 orange
1 teaspoon vanilla extract
300 g (10½ oz) thick
  (double/heavy) cream
2 tablespoons amaretto or other
  almond-flavoured liqueur (optional)
75 g (2¾ oz/1½ cups) small almond
  biscotti, coarsely chopped

Combine the cherries and 115 g (4 oz/½ cup) of the caster sugar in a small saucepan, cover, then slowly bring to the boil. Cook the mixture, stirring occasionally, for 5–6 minutes over medium–low heat or until the cherries have softened and given up their juices.

Combine the cornflour with 1 tablespoon water in a small bowl and stir until a smooth paste forms. Stirring constantly, add the cornflour mixture to the simmering cherries. Cook, stirring, for 1 minute or until the cherry liquid has boiled and thickened slightly. Remove from the heat and cool to room temperature. Transfer to a bowl, cover, then refrigerate for 1 hour or until chilled.

Meanwhile, combine the cream cheese, orange rind, vanilla and the remaining sugar in a bowl and, using electric beaters, beat until mixture is smooth and fluffy. Add the cream and beat for 2–3 minutes or until mixture is thick and smooth, then stir in the amaretto, if using. Transfer the cream to a bowl, cover and refrigerate for 1 hour or until well chilled.

To assemble the parfait, divide half the cherries among six 250 ml (9 fl oz/1 cup) capacity glasses, then spoon half the cream cheese mixture over cherries. Scatter half the biscotti crumbs over cream cheese, then repeat layering, finishing with a layer of crumbs. Serve immediately.

When cherries are in season use fresh cherries instead; buy 700 g (1 lb 9 oz) and pit them using a cherry pitter. Both cherry mixture and cream cheese mixture can be prepared up to a day in advance and refrigerated; crumbs can be made and kept in an airtight container up to a day in advance, too. Assembling the dessert takes just a few minutes.

Pineapple in star-anise syrup with coconut ice cream

100 g (3½ oz/¾ cup) shaved palm
  sugar (jaggery)
2 star anise
2 tablespoons lime juice, plus
  ½ teaspoon finely grated lime rind
1 small sweet pineapple, skinned,
  cored and thinly sliced
20 g (¾ oz/⅓ cup) shredded
  coconut, toasted
1 litre (35 fl oz) vanilla ice cream

Combine the palm sugar with 125 ml (4 fl oz/ ½ cup) water in a small saucepan. Add the star anise, then stir over medium heat for 3–4 minutes or until the sugar dissolves. Bring to the boil and cook for 6 minutes or until the syrup is reduced by half. Remove from the heat and stir in the lime juice and grated rind.

Meanwhile, place the pineapple in a heatproof bowl. Place the coconut in a shallow plate and roll 4 large scoops of ice cream in the coconut until well coated with the coconut. Refreeze ice cream balls until ready to serve.

Pour the warm syrup over the pineapple and stand until cooled to room temperature. Divide the pineapple and syrup among plates, top each with a ball of ice cream and serve immediately.

Preparation time: 15 minutes   **Cooking time:** 10 minutes   **Serves:** 4

Preparation time: 20 minutes
plus at least 2 hours chilling time and
30 minutes standing time

Cooking time: 35 minutes

Serves: 6

Chocolate-caramel tarts

butter, for greasing
1½ tablespoons caster
(superfine) sugar
2 sheets frozen shortcrust (pie)
pastry, thawed

Caramel

230 g (8 oz/1 cup) caster
(superfine) sugar
75 g (2½ oz) unsalted butter,
chopped
80 ml (2½ fl oz/⅓ cup) cream

Chocolate topping

80 ml (2½ fl oz/⅓ cup) cream
150 g (5½ oz) dark chocolate
(70% cocoa solids), chopped

Preheat the oven to 180°C (350°F/Gas 4). Lightly grease six 10 cm (4 inch) wide, 2 cm (¾ inch) deep fluted tartlet tins. Sprinkle the pastry evenly with the caster sugar. Using a 10 cm (4 inch) round cutter, cut out 6 rounds. Line each tin with a circle of pastry, pressing pastry gently to cover sides of tins. Prick the bases with a fork. Place in the freezer for 5 minutes. Line the bases with baking paper, pour in some baking beads or uncooked rice and bake for 10–12 minutes. Remove the paper and beads and bake for another 5 minutes or until light golden. Cool.

To make the caramel, combine 60 ml (2 fl oz/¼ cup) water and sugar in a heavy-based saucepan over medium heat. Cook without stirring for 10–15 minutes or until the mixture turns a medium caramel colour. Working quickly, remove the pan from the heat and add the butter and cream; take care as the mixture will spit. Swirl the pan to combine well, then divide the caramel among the cooled pastry cases. Refrigerate for at least 2 hours or until the caramel has set.

To make the chocolate topping, bring the cream to the boil in a small saucepan over medium heat. Add the chocolate, remove the pan from the heat and stir to combine well. Stand for 5 minutes or until the chocolate has melted, then whisk the mixture until smooth. Cool slightly, then pour over the caramel in the pastry cases. Refrigerate until the chocolate has set. Remove from the refrigerator 30 minutes before serving.

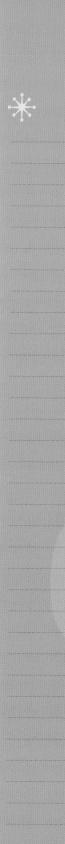

Spiced wine jelly

600 ml (21 fl oz) red wine
500 ml (17 fl oz/2 cups) apple
  and blackcurrant juice
220 g (7¾ oz/1 cup) caster
  (superfine) sugar
2 cinnamon sticks
1 teaspoon whole cloves
4 cardamom pods, lightly crushed
3 wide strips orange zest, all white
  pith removed
1½ tablespoons powdered gelatine
vanilla ice cream, to serve (optional)

Combine the red wine, 400 ml (14 fl oz) of the juice, sugar, spices and zest in a saucepan and slowly bring nearly to the boil. Remove from the heat, cover and stand for 30 minutes to allow the flavours to develop, then cool to room temperature.

Meanwhile, sprinkle the gelatine over the remaining juice in a small heatproof bowl and stand for 5 minutes or until the gelatine has softened. Place the bowl in a small saucepan, add warm water to come halfway up the side of the bowl, then place over medium–low heat for 5–6 minutes or until the gelatine has dissolved. Strain the wine mixture, discarding solids, then stir in the gelatine mixture. Divide among six 200 ml (7 fl oz) moulds, cover and refrigerate for 3 hours or until firm.

To serve, dip each jelly mould briefly into a bowl of hot water to loosen jelly, then turn out onto serving plates or shallow bowls. Serve immediately, with a scoop of ice cream alongside, if using.

Preparation time: 30 minutes
plus 3 hours chilling time

Cooking time: 10 minutes

Serves: 6

Preparation time: 50 minutes
plus overnight chilling and
at least 1 hour standing time

Cooking time: 50 minutes

Serves: 6–8

Hazelnut vacherin with chocolate-coffee cream

90 g (3¼ oz/¾ cup) ground hazelnuts
3 egg whites, at room temperature
180 g (6 oz/¾ cup) caster
  (superfine) sugar
45 g (1½ oz/⅓ cup) roasted hazelnuts,
  roughly chopped

Chocolate-coffee cream
300 g (10½ oz) dark chocolate,
  finely chopped
300 ml (10½ fl oz) cream
1 tablespoon instant coffee

Preheat the oven to 160°C (315°F/Gas 2–3).
Line 2 baking trays with baking paper and draw
2 rectangles 10 x 25 cm (4 x 10 inches) on each
piece of paper, allowing a little room for spreading.
Place the ground hazelnuts in a small frying pan
and stir over medium heat for about 2–3 minutes
or until fragrant, then remove from heat and cool.

Whisk the egg whites in a small bowl with an
electric mixer until soft peaks form. Whisking
constantly, add the sugar, a little at a time,
whisking well between additions, then whisk for
a few minutes until mixture is thick and glossy.
Gently fold in the ground hazelnuts. Using a
palette knife, spread the meringue mixture evenly
over the 4 rectangles. Sprinkle the chopped
hazelnuts over the top of one of the rectangles.
Bake meringues for 45 minutes or until dry to
touch. Turn oven off and leave meringues in the
oven to cool and dry out completely.

To make the chocolate-coffee cream, place
the chocolate in a heatproof bowl. Place the
cream and coffee in a saucepan, bring to the
boil, then remove from heat and pour over the
chocolate. Stand for 30 seconds, then stir
gently until the chocolate has melted. Allow to
set. When set, beat the chocolate mixture with
electric beaters for about 30 seconds or until
just lightened in texture slightly; do not overbeat
or the mixture will curdle.

When cool, place one of the plain meringues
on a serving platter. Spread with a third of the
chocolate-coffee cream, then top with another
plain rectangle of meringue. Repeat with the
remaining cream and meringues, finishing with
the nut-topped meringue. Cover with plastic wrap
and refrigerate overnight. Remove from the fridge
1–2 hours before serving, to allow to soften.

Lime and coconut shortcakes

Raspberry or plum jam can be used instead of the lime marmalade as can lemon curd, if you prefer. The desiccated coconut in the shortcake dough can be replaced with ground almonds and slivered or chopped almonds can be used to decorate, instead of the shredded coconut. Custard, either homemade or purchased, is also a good accompaniment.

45 g (1½ oz/¾ cup) shredded coconut
150 g (5½ oz) unsalted butter, chopped, plus extra, for greasing
250 g (9 oz/1⅔ cups) plain (all-purpose) flour, plus extra, for dusting
2 teaspoons baking powder
115 g (4 oz/½ cup) caster (superfine) sugar
65 g (2½ oz/¾ cup) desiccated coconut
1 egg, lightly beaten
1 teaspoon coconut essence
210 g (7½ oz/⅔ cup) lime marmalade
softly whipped cream, to serve

Preheat the oven to 170°C (325°F/Gas 3). Spread the shredded coconut on a baking tray and toast in oven for 6–7 minutes or until light golden. Cool coconut and set aside.

Lightly grease and flour 6 holes of a standard non-stick muffin or friand tin. Line the holes with a circle of baking paper. Sift the flour and baking powder into a bowl, then stir in the sugar and desiccated coconut. Rub in butter until mixture resembles coarse breadcrumbs. Make a well in the centre, add the egg and coconut essence and, using a fork, stir egg into flour mixture until a coarse dough forms. Turn out on a lightly floured board and knead briefly until smooth.

Take about 2 heaped tablespoons of the dough and, using your hands, form into a flat circle about 5 mm (¼ inch) thick. Use the circle to line one of the muffin holes, trimming edges. Repeat until the 6 muffin holes are lined with dough. Place 1 tablespoon of marmalade in each. Divide the remaining dough, including any trimmings, into 6 even pieces and press each piece into a round large enough to cover each shortcake. Press the edges of the pastry together to seal, then bake for 20 minutes or until pastry is golden. Cool the shortcakes in the muffin tin for 10 minutes, then carefully turn out onto a wire rack to serve or to cool completely.

To serve, place shortcakes on serving plates, add a generous dollop of cream and sprinkle with toasted coconut.

Preparation time: 30 minutes　　**Cooking time:** 30 minutes　　**Serves:** 6

Preparation time: 30 minutes
plus 2 hours chilling time

Cooking time: 40 minutes

Serves: 6

Berry sago pudding

750 g (1 lb 10 oz/6 cups) frozen
  mixed berries
65 g (2½ oz/⅓ cup) sago
230 g (8 oz/1 cup) caster
  (superfine) sugar
whipped cream, to serve

Combine the berries and 125 ml (4 fl oz/
½ cup) water in a saucepan, cover and cook
over medium heat for 10 minutes or until the
berries are soft and have given up all their
juices. Strain berries in a colander placed over
a bowl, pressing berries gently to extract as
much liquid as possible. Reserve solids. Measure
the juice, then make the quantity up to 625 ml
(21½ fl oz/2½ cups) with water.

Combine the berry liquid with the sago in a
saucepan, then bring to the boil, stirring often,
over medium–low heat. Cover, reduce heat to
low and cook, stirring often, for 30 minutes or
until sago is soft and translucent and mixture
has thickened. Take care that mixture does not
stick to the base of the pan. Add the sugar, stir
until dissolved, then remove from heat. Cool the
berry sago to room temperature, then stir in the
reserved berry solids. Transfer to a bowl, cover
and refrigerate for 2 hours or until chilled. Divide
the mixture among serving bowls or glasses, top
with whipped cream and serve.

**Presentation transforms an old-
fashioned favourite. We've used
green Depression-era glasses.**

Rice flour pudding with rhubarb-rosewater compote

Strawberries can be used in the compote if you prefer. Use 500 g (1 lb 2 oz) hulled strawberries, cut into thick slices, and 110 g (3¾ oz/½ cup) caster (superfine) sugar. Combine these in a saucepan, cover, then bring slowly to the boil over medium–low heat. Cook for 2–3 minutes or until strawberries have released their juices, then thicken slightly with 2 teaspoons cornflour (cornstarch). Add rosewater to taste, or try it with orange blossom water instead.

600 ml (21 fl oz) milk
115 g (4 oz/½ cup) caster
   (superfine) sugar
1 cinnamon stick
3 cardamom pods, crushed
3 x 1 cm (½ inch) wide strips
   orange zest
60 g (2¼ oz/⅓ cup) rice flour
1½ tablespoons cornflour (cornstarch)
chopped pistachios, to serve (optional)

Rhubarb-rosewater compote
450 g (1 lb) rhubarb (about 1 bunch)
   trimmed and cut into 1 cm
   (½ inch) pieces
80 ml (2½ fl oz/⅓ cup) orange juice
115 g (4 oz/½ cup) caster
   (superfine) sugar
½ teaspoon rosewater, or to taste

To make the rhubarb-rosewater compote, combine rhubarb, orange juice and sugar in a saucepan over medium heat. Cover, bring to the boil, reduce heat to low and cook for 3–4 minutes or until sugar has dissolved and rhubarb has softened. Cool to room temperature, then stir in rosewater. Transfer to a bowl, cover and refrigerate.

Meanwhile, combine 500 ml (17 fl oz/2 cups) of the milk, sugar, cinnamon, cardamom and orange zest in a saucepan and slowly bring almost to the boil over a low heat, stirring to dissolve sugar. Remove mixture from heat, cover and stand for 30 minutes to allow flavours to infuse. Strain mixture, discarding solids. Combine remaining milk with rice flour and cornflour in a small bowl and stir to form a smooth paste. Reheat the strained milk mixture in a saucepan over medium heat, bring to the boil, then whisking constantly, add the rice flour paste. Cook mixture, whisking constantly, for 5 minutes or until it comes back to the boil. Reduce heat to low and cook, whisking constantly to avoid lumps forming, for 3 minutes or until thick and smooth. Remove from heat and cool slightly, whisking occasionally to prevent lumps or a skin forming. Cool slightly, then divide among four 300 ml (10½ fl oz) serving glasses or bowls. Cover and chill for about 1 hour or until set.

To serve, spoon the rhubarb mixture over the rice puddings, sprinkle with the pistachios, if using, and serve.

Preparation time: 20 minutes
plus 30 minutes standing time
and 1 hour chilling time

Cooking time: 20 minutes

Serves: 4

Preparation time: 20 minutes
plus 4 hours chilling time

Cooking time: 3 hours 10 minutes

Serves: 6–8

Apple terrine

145 g (5½ oz/⅔ cup) caster
  (superfine) sugar
1.5 kg (3 lb 5 oz) granny smith apples
  (about 9), peeled and cored
finely grated rind of 1 lemon
2 teaspoons ground cinnamon
1 tablespoon honey
250 g (9 oz/1 cup) Greek-style yoghurt

Preheat the oven to 160°C (315°F/Gas 2–3).
Line a 21 x 8 x 9 cm (8¼ x 3¼ x 3½ inch) loaf
(bar) tin with a layer of foil and a layer
of baking paper, overhanging long sides by
10 cm (4 inches).

Combine 90 g (3¼ oz/⅓ cup) of the sugar
and 2 tablespoons water in a small saucepan,
place over low heat and swirl the pan until
the sugar and water are combined. Cook for
6–8 minutes or until the sugar is golden, swirling
the pan every couple of minutes to distribute
the heat. Pour the caramel into the loaf tin,
taking care as the caramel is very hot, then stand
for 20 minutes or until the caramel has cooled.

Meanwhile, thinly slice the apples and
combine with the remaining sugar, lemon rind
and cinnamon in a large bowl. Layer the apple
slices on top of the cooled caramel in the tin,
packing them in very tightly. Enclose the apple
with the overhanging foil and baking paper, then
wrap tin in foil to secure. Bake for 3 hours or
until apples are golden and very tender. Cool
terrine completely, then refrigerate for 4 hours
or until chilled.

Combine the honey and yoghurt in a bowl and
refrigerate until ready to serve.

To serve, turn the terrine out onto a platter,
cut into slices using a sharp serrated knife and
serve with the yoghurt. The terrine can be served
chilled or at room temperature.

Peach and nutmeg crème brûlée

If peaches are in season, use 260 g
(9¼ oz/1 cup) chopped ripe peaches
instead of tinned peaches. You could
also use nectarines, apricots or
even pitted fresh cherries. For best
results, when caramelising the sugar,
use a small blow torch. The process
is much faster and stops the custard
softening too much under the heat of
the grill. If you need to use the oven
grill, place ramekins in a baking dish
and pack ice around them to help
keep the custard cool under the grill.

1 x 410 g (14½ oz) tin sliced peaches
    in natural juice, drained well
8 egg yolks
110 g (3¾ oz/½ cup) caster
    (superfine) sugar
1 teaspoon freshly grated nutmeg
1½ teaspoons natural vanilla extract
750 g (1 lb 10 oz/3 cups) thick
    (double/heavy) cream
60 g (2¼ oz/¼ cup) demerara sugar

Preheat the oven to 150°C (300°F/Gas 2). Place
six 185 ml (6 fl oz/¾ cup) capacity ovenproof
ramekins or teacups into a roasting pan. Pat the
peaches dry on paper towels to remove excess
liquid, then coarsely chop. Divide the peaches
among the ramekins or teacups.

Combine the yolks, caster sugar, nutmeg and
vanilla in a bowl and whisk until combined well.

Bring the cream almost to the boil in a
saucepan over medium heat, then pour over
the egg mixture and whisk until well combined.
Pour the mixture into ramekins or teacups, then
pour boiling water into the roasting pan to come
halfway up the sides of the ramekins or teacups.
Bake for 30–40 minutes or until just set; the
centres will still be a little wobbly. Remove
ramekins or teacups from the pan, cool to room
temperature, cover and refrigerate for 4 hours or
overnight to set.

Preheat oven grill (broiler) to high. Divide
demerara sugar among brûlées, sprinkling it
in an even layer. Place brûlées under the grill,
3 cm (1¼ inches) from the heat source, for
2 minutes or until sugar melts and caramelises.
Serve immediately.

Preparation time: 20 minutes
plus 4 hours chilling time

Cooking time: 40 minutes

Serves: 6

Preparation time: 20 minutes   Cooking time: 40 minutes   Serves: 4–6

Pear, almond and elderflower crumble

125 ml (4 fl oz/½ cup) elderflower cordial

1.1 kg (2 lb 7 oz) firm ripe William pears (about 6), peeled and cored

100 g (3½ oz) unsalted butter, chopped, plus extra for greasing

110 g (3¾ oz/¾ cup) plain (all-purpose) flour

½ teaspoon ground cardamom

95 g (3¼ oz/½ cup lightly packed) brown sugar

80 g (2¾ oz/½ cup) chopped almonds

cream or vanilla ice cream, to serve

Combine the cordial and 125 ml (4 fl oz/½ cup) water in a large deep saucepan and bring to the boil over medium–low heat. Chop the pears into 2 cm (¾ inch) cubes and add to the syrup. Cook for 7 minutes or until pear is almost tender. Using a slotted spoon, transfer the pear to a plate and leave to cool. Place in a shallow, greased 1.5 litre (52 fl oz/6 cup) capacity ovenproof dish.

Preheat the oven to 180°C (350°F/Gas 4).

Sift the flour, cardamom, sugar and a pinch of salt into a large bowl. Rub in the butter using your fingertips until the mixture resembles coarse breadcrumbs. Stir in the almonds, then sprinkle the mixture over the pear.

Bake for 30 minutes or until the topping is golden and crisp.

Serve warm with cream or vanilla ice cream.

If fresh pears are not available, use tinned pears in their natural juice. Place drained, chopped pears in prepared ovenproof dish and sprinkle with 80 ml (2½ fl oz/⅓ cup) elderflower cordial. Leave to stand for 10 minutes before adding crumble topping. Elderflower cordial is available from selected delis and supermarkets. Cool, strain and refrigerate remaining elderflower syrup in an airtight container for up to 1 week. This syrup is delicious spooned over fresh lychees, melon, pineapple or grapes.

Gingerbread soufflé

120 g (4¼ oz) unsalted butter,
  plus extra for greasing
20 g (¾ oz) caster (superfine) sugar,
  for dusting soufflé cups
100 g (3½ oz/⅔ cup) plain
  (all-purpose) flour
125 ml (4 fl oz/½ cup) milk
125 ml (4 fl oz/½ cup) cream
5 large eggs, separated
280 g (10 oz/1½ cups lightly packed)
  brown sugar
1 tablespoon ground ginger
1 teaspoon cinnamon
300 g (10½ oz) thick
  (double/heavy) cream
2 tablespoons brandy
2 teaspoons icing (confectioner's)
  sugar, for dusting

Preheat the oven to 200°C (400°F/Gas 6). Lightly grease six 250 ml (9 fl oz/1 cup) capacity ramekins. Pour a little caster sugar into each, swirling to coat inside of ramekins and shaking out excess. Place ramekins on a baking paper-lined baking tray and set aside.

Melt the butter in a saucepan over medium heat, add the flour, stirring to combine well, then cook, stirring constantly, for 1 minute. Combine the milk and cream in a jug and gradually stir into the flour mixture. Stirring constantly to prevent lumps forming, cook for 3–4 minutes or until the mixture thickens. Transfer the mixture to a large bowl and whisk in the egg yolks, one at a time.

Combine the brown sugar with the spices and gradually whisk into the egg mixture until smooth. Set aside.

Beat the egg whites until firm peaks form, then stir a third of the egg whites into the milk mixture to loosen it a little. Then, very gently and gradually, fold the remaining egg whites into the milk mixture.

Reduce the oven temperature to 180°C (350°F/Gas 4). Divide the soufflé mixture among the ramekins and run your finger along the inside of each one to create a small ridge. Bake for 30–35 minutes or until the soufflés have risen above the dish.

Meanwhile, combine the cream and brandy in a small bowl and whisk until soft peaks form.

Dust the soufflés with the icing sugar and serve immediately, with the brandy cream passed separately.

Preparation time: 30 minutes   **Cooking time:** 40 minutes   **Serves:** 6

Preparation time: 50 minutes
plus 50 minutes chilling time

Cooking time: 1 hour 20 minutes

Serves: 6–8

Vanilla rice tart with apricot purée

80 g (2¾ oz) cold butter, chopped,
   plus extra for greasing
225 g (8 oz/1½ cups) plain
   (all-purpose) flour
30 g (1 oz/¼ cup) icing (confectioner's)
   sugar, plus extra, for dusting
1 egg yolk

Vanilla rice filling

110 g (3¾ oz/½ cup) short-grain rice
250 ml (9 fl oz/1 cup) milk
300 ml (10½ fl oz/1¼ cups) cream
60 g (2¼ oz/¼ cup) caster
   (superfine) sugar
1 teaspoon natural vanilla extract
2 egg yolks
100 g (3½ oz) ricotta cheese

Apricot purée

100 g (3½ oz/¾ cup) dried
   apricots, chopped
1½ tablespoons caster
   (superfine) sugar
¼ teaspoon ground cinnamon

Grease a shallow 22 cm (8½ inch) round fluted flan tin with a removable base. Place the flour, butter and sugar in a food processor and process until the mixture resembles breadcrumbs. Add the egg yolk and about 1 tablespoon of iced water, then using the pulse button, briefly process until the mixture just comes together. Turn onto a lightly floured surface and gather into a ball. Wrap in plastic wrap and refrigerate for 20 minutes.

Roll the pastry between 2 sheets of baking paper lightly dusted with flour until large enough to line base and side of tin. Remove the baking paper, lift the pastry into the tin, easing it in to fit, then trim off any excess. Prick the base with a fork. Line with baking paper and fill with baking beads or rice. Refrigerate for 30 minutes. Meanwhile, preheat the oven to 180°C (350°F/ Gas 4). Bake pastry shell for 10 minutes. Remove the beads and paper and bake for another 10 minutes or until dry and light golden.

To make the vanilla rice filling, combine the rice, milk and 125 ml (4 fl oz/½ cup) of the cream in a saucepan. Stir over medium heat until the mixture comes to the boil. Reduce heat to low, cover and cook for about 15 minutes, stirring occasionally, until the rice is nearly tender and the mixture is thick. Remove from the heat, stir in the sugar and vanilla, then cool. Stir in the egg yolks, ricotta and remaining cream. Pour the rice mixture into the prepared pastry case. Bake for 30–35 minutes or until the mixture is just set.

To make the apricot purée, combine the apricots, 175 ml (5½ fl oz/¾ cup) water, sugar and cinnamon in a small saucepan and bring to the boil over medium heat. Reduce heat to low and cook for 5 minutes or until soft. Remove from heat and allow to cool. Process until smooth. If mixture is very thick, add a little extra water.

Remove the tart from the oven and cool to room temperature. Dust with icing sugar and serve in wedges with the apricot purée.

Banana semifreddo with rum-caramel sauce

3 large egg yolks
125 g (4½ oz/⅔ cup, lightly packed)
  brown sugar
60 ml (2 fl oz/¼ cup) dark rum
180 g (6 oz/¾ cup) mashed very ripe
  banana (about 1)
2 teaspoons lime or lemon juice
200 ml (7 fl oz) cream, whipped
2 large egg whites, at room temperature

Rum-caramel sauce
170 g (6 oz/⅔ cup) caster
  (superfine) sugar
2 tablespoons unsalted butter
2 tablespoons dark rum
125 ml (4 fl oz/½ cup) cream

Have ready a large bowl with 3 cups of ice
and 500 ml (17 fl oz/2 cups) cold water in it.
Combine the egg yolks, sugar and rum in a metal
bowl. Whisk to combine well, then, whisking
continuously, set bowl over a saucepan of boiling
water and whisk for 10–12 minutes or until thick
and pale. Transfer the bowl to the ice bath and
continue whisking until cold.

Combine the banana and lime juice in
a bowl, stirring to mix well, then fold in the
whipped cream.

In a large clean bowl whisk the egg whites
and a pinch of salt until firm peaks form. Gently
fold the banana mixture into the cooled egg-yolk
mixture. Fold a third of the egg whites into the
egg-yolk mixture to loosen, then gently fold in
the remaining egg white. Divide mixture among
six 125 ml (4 fl oz/½ cup) capacity glasses or
ceramic ramekins. Cover and freeze for 4 hours
or overnight.

To make the rum-caramel sauce, combine
sugar and 100 ml (3½ fl oz) water in a small
heavy-based saucepan over a medium–high
heat, stirring until sugar dissolves. Bring to
the boil, then reduce heat to low and cook for
5–10 minutes or until caramelised. Remove from
the heat and, taking care as mixture will spit,
stir in the butter, rum and cream. Return
the saucepan to a low heat and stir the sauce
continuously until smooth. Cool completely.

Serve the banana semifreddo topped with the
rum-caramel sauce.

Preparation time: 30 minutes
plus at least 4 hours chilling time

Cooking time: 10 minutes

Serves: 6

INDEX

Published in 2010 by Murdoch Books Pty Limited

Murdoch Books Australia
Pier 8/9
23 Hickson Road
Millers Point NSW 2000
Phone: +61 (0) 2 8220 2000
Fax: +61 (0) 2 8220 2558
www.murdochbooks.com.au

Murdoch Books UK Limited
Erico House, 6th Floor
93–99 Upper Richmond Road
Putney, London SW15 2TG
Phone: +44 (0) 20 8785 5995
Fax: +44 (0) 20 8785 5985
www.murdochbooks.co.uk

Publishing director: Kay Scarlett
Project editor: Kristin Buesing
Copy editor: Micaela Di Piramo
Food editor: Leanne Kitchen
Cover concept: Yolande Gray
Design concept: Emilia Toia
Photographer: Natasha Milne
Stylist: Kate Brown
Food preparation: Kirrily La Rosa
Recipes developed by Peta Dent, Michelle Earl, Heidi Flett, Fiona Hammond, Vicky Harris, Leanne Kitchen, Kathy Knudsen, Barbara Lowery, Kim Meredith, Wendy Quisumbing, Angela Tregonning and the Murdoch Books test kitchen.

National Library of Australia Cataloguing-in-Publication Data
Title: Easy Gourmet.
ISBN: 9781741964417 (pbk.)
Series: My Kitchen series.
Notes: Includes index.
Subjects: Quick and easy cookery
Dewey Number: 641.552
A catalogue record for this book is available from the British Library.

PRINTED IN CHINA.

IMPORTANT: Those who might be at risk from the effects of salmonella poisoning (the elderly, pregnant women, young children and those suffering from immune deficiency diseases) should consult their doctor with any concerns about eating raw eggs.

OVEN GUIDE: You may find cooking times vary depending on the oven you are using. For fan-forced ovens, as a general rule, set the oven temperature to 20°C (35°F) lower than indicated in the recipe.